NEW WOMAN WRITERS

NEW WOMAN WRITERS

Lyssa Randolph
&
Marion Shaw

NORTHCOTE
BRITISH
COUNCIL

© Copyright 2007 by Lyssa Randolph and Marion Shaw

First published in 2007 by Northcote House Publishers Ltd, Horndon, Tavistock, Devon, PL19 9NQ, United Kingdom.
Tel: +44 (01822) 810066. Fax: +44 (01822) 810034.

British Library Cataloguing-in-Publication Data
A catalogue record for this book is available from the British Library

ISBN 978-0-7463-1079-3 hardcover
ISBN 978-0-7463-1084-7 paperback

Typeset by TW Typesetting, Plymouth, Devon
Printed and bound by CPI Group (UK) Ltd, Croydon, CR0 4YY

For
Maureen and Simon Randolph

Contents

Preface

Innovative, radical, satirical, polemical: the wide-ranging and engaging nature of New Woman writing has received extensive study in the last decade, developing a scholarship which has reassessed its significant contribution to modern literary culture and gender politics. Of necessity this volume provides only a brief introduction to a very ideologically and stylistically diverse group of writers, with a focus on the novels, short stories, plays and some non-fiction by more prominent women writers. We have chosen to exclude New Woman poets from this study, a group who include Michael Field, Amy Levy, Alice Meynell, Constance Naden and Mary F. Robinson. However, their literary contribution was a significant one and integral to feminist identities and to the contemporary culture.

New Woman fiction will be treated as a female-authored genre, but will take into account the work of male contemporaries, particularly as regards drama. Both female and male interlocutors are read as an important dialectic in the consideration of the way in which feminist ideas were established and contested in the literary culture. Chapter 1 provides an overview of the women's movement between 1880 and 1910, and considers the diversity of feminist and female identities and lifestyles and the kinds of campaigns that the New Woman was involved in. Chapter 2 looks at the representation of the woman artist in the context of debates on literary value and its relationship to gender and genre. Chapter 3 considers some texts by a number of women writers. New readings of novels, critical work and short stories give attention to the themes of motherhood, sexuality and the close engagement of New Woman fiction with evolutionary science and eugenics, and their relationship to imperialism. Brief details of New Woman writers' lives can be found in the Biographical Outlines. Drama has received less critical attention than other writing by New Women. The final chapter seeks to remedy this and extends the *fin-de-siècle* period in order to look at suffrage and other drama, with a focus on the leading woman playwright of the Edwardian era, Elizabeth Robins. The dramatic expression of themes addressed in the previous chapters is further explored here, especially motherhood and the emergence of women from sexual and domestic dependency. We hope that readers will make use of the Annotated Bibliography which is intended to provide a useful starting point for further study and research in the field.

Biographical Outlines

This book departs from the convention of most other studies in the Writers and their Work series in that it does not focus on a single author. Instead, its subject is a number of authors identified as New Woman writers. We offer brief histories of ten women writing at the turn of the nineteenth century upon whom the study concentrates.

Emma Frances Brooke (c. 1844–1926) was born in Cheshire and was educated at Newnham College, Cambridge. She moved to London in 1879, where she mixed in intellectual circles including Eleanor Marx, Olive Schreiner, Havelock Ellis and Edward Carpenter. She attended the Men and Women Club in London and had an extensive involvement in the Fabian Society and its politics. Under the pseudonym of E. Fairfax Byrnne she wrote, *A Fair Country Maid* (1883) *Entangled* (1885) and *The Heir without a Heritage* (1887). William Heinemann published Brooke's *A Superfluous Woman* (1894), *Life the Accuser* (1896) and *Transition* (1895) which featured a central character who was based on Sidney Webb. She discussed and wrote on women's economic independence and the payment of mothers; Grant Richards published her *Tabulation of the Factory Laws* (1898) on labour law. The novels *The Confession of Stephen Whapshare* (1898), *The Engrafted Rose* (1899) and *The House of Robershaye* (1912) followed.

Katherine Mannington (Hunt) Caffyn ('Iota') (1855–1926) was born in Ireland. She trained as a nurse at St Thomas Hospital in London. In 1879 she married a surgeon, also a best-selling novelist, and emigrated a year later to Australia with him and their baby. They returned to live in London some years later. Her novels include *A Yellow Aster* (1894), *A Comedy in Spasms* (1895) and *Anne Mauleverer* (1899).

Alice Mona (Alison) Caird (1854–1932) was born on the Isle of Wight to Matilda Ann Jane Hector and John Alison, landowner and engineer. She married James Alexander Caird of a Scottish landowning family, in London in 1877. Their only child, Alister James was born in 1884. Mona Caird divided her time between the estate at Cassencary on the Cree on the south-west coast of Scotland, and the intellectual life of London, including a close friendship with the writers Elizabeth and William Sharp. She published short stories, *Some Whims of Fate* (1896) and *The Crook of the Bough* (1898), as well as articles and pamphlets on anti-vivisection, marriage and pacifism. There are seven, attributed, novels: *The Wing of Azrael* (1889); *A Romance of the Moors* (1891); *The Daughters of Danaus* (1894); *The Pathways of the Gods* (1898); *Love and His Mask* (1901); *The Stones of Sacrifice* (1915), and *The Great Wave* (1931).

Frances Elizabeth Bellenden (Clarke) McFall (Sarah Grand) (1854–1943) was born in Donaghadee, County Down in Ireland, to Edward John Bellenden Clarke and Margaret Bell née Sherwood. At the age of seven, after her father's death, the family of five children moved with their mother to Yorkshire. In 1871 Grand married a widowed army surgeon, David Chambers McFall, who had two sons, Haldane and Albert, aged ten and eight; their only child together, David Archibald Edward McFall was born the same year. They travelled extensively in the Far East and in Europe. Her first book, *Two Dear Little Feet* was published in 1873. Grand printed her first novel, *Ideala: A Study from Life* (1888) herself several years after its completion. She left her husband, and her son, Archie, in 1890. After the early novels, *A Domestic Experiment* (1891) and *Singularly Deluded* (1892), she reinvented herself as 'Madame' Sarah Grand and published *The Heavenly Twins* (1893) in three volumes. Collected short stories were published in *Our Manifold Nature* (1894), and Grand also contributed articles to, and was interviewed in, many periodicals. In the late 1890s, she was a member of the Women Writers' Suffrage League, lecturing and campaigning widely in England and America. Her last books were *Adnam's Orchard* (1912), its sequel *The Winged Victory* (1916) and short stories, *Variety* (1922). She served as Mayoress of Bath from 1922 to 1929.

Annie Sophie Cory (1868–1952) was also known as Vivian Cory, and took the pen name of Victoria Cross(e). She was born at Rawalpindi in Punjab, to Fanny (Griffin) and Arthur Cory. Her father was an officer in the Bengal army, editor of the Civil and Military Gazette of Lahore and a critic of British policy. Cross grew up in Karachi and lived for many years in India. Her novels include *The Woman Who Didn't* (1895); *Anna Lombard* (1901); *Six Chapters of a Man's Life* (1903); *Life's Shop Window* (1907); *Five Nights* (1908); *Over Life's Edge* (1921) and short stories, *Daughters of Heaven* (1920). She died in Italy in 1952.

Menie Muriel Dowie (1867–1945) was born in Liverpool, the second daughter of James Muir Dowie, a Liverpool merchant, and Annie Dowie, and the granddaughter of Robert Chambers (founder of *Chambers' Dictionary* and author of *Vestiges of Creation*). During her girlhood she was educated in Stuttgart and France, and enjoyed fishing and hunting in the Scottish Highlands. *A Girl in the Karpathians* (1890), the account of her horseback travels as a single woman in the mountains, brought her celebrity as she lectured to London audiences. In 1891 she married Henry Norman, a travel writer; they travelled extensively together. Their son, Henry was born in 1897. A regular contributor to *The Daily Chronicle* and other periodicals, she edited a collection of biographical essays, *Women Adventurers* (1893) and her first novel *Gallia* was published by Methuen two years later. She contributed short stories to *The Yellow Book* and *Chambers' Journal*, but wrote only two more novels, *The Crook of the Bough* (1898) and *Love and His Mask* (1901), as well as the short story volume, *Some Whims of Fate* (1896). In 1903 she was divorced by Henry Norman on grounds of adultery with Edward Fitzgerald, whom she married later that year; Henry Norman was awarded custody of their child. She continued to travel, took up farming in the 1920s and became a cattle breeder on her farm near Chichester.

Mary Chavelita Dunne (George Egerton) (1859–1945) was born in Melbourne, Australia; she spent much of her childhood in

Ireland with her Irish father; her Welsh mother died when she was 14. She attended school in Germany. After trying nursing in London, she moved to New York for two years, then returned to England. She had an affair with the bigamous Henry Higginson and they bought a house in Norway. The violent and alcoholic Higginson died two years later. In 1891 she married Newfoundlander, George Egerton Clairmonte, a young novelist. She moved from their home in County Cork to London in 1894. Soon after the birth of their son, George, in 1895, the relationship ended, and they were divorced in 1901. She met a theatre agent, Reginald Golding Bright, fifteen years her junior, whom she married in 1901. Her oeuvre includes story collections, *Keynotes* (1893), *Discords* (1894), *Symphonies* (1897); *Fantasias* (1898); her only novel, *The Wheel of God* (1898); prose fiction, *Rosa Amorosa* (1901), *Flies in Amber* (1905); and the plays, *His Wife's Family* (1907), *The Backsliders* (1910) and *Camilla States Her Case* (1925).

Violet Paget (Vernon Lee) (1856–1935) was born in France; her early childhood was spent in Germany. She studied in Italy and continued to spend most of her life there. Her half brother, Eugene Lee Hamilton, was also a published writer. Lee enjoyed a long writing career including essays, short stories, books about travel, art, the Renaissance, and what she considered to be her most important writing, on aesthetics. Works on aesthetics include, *Juvenilia: Essays on Sundry Aesthetical Questions 2 vols* (1881); *Limbo and Other Essays* (1897); and *The Beautiful: An Introduction to Psychological Aesthetics* (1913). Travel books include *Genius Loci* (1899) and *The Spirit of Rome* (1906). Her relationship with Clementina (Kit) Anstruther Thomson included collaborative work, resulting in the study *Beauty and Ugliness and Other Studies in Psychological Aesthetics* (1897; 1912). Violet enjoyed an intense, loving relationship with the poet, Mary A. F. Robinson from 1880 to 1886, until Mary's engagement. Critics such as Terry Castle and Kathy Psomiades have described Lee as a lesbian writer using lesbian aesthetics.

Elizabeth Robins (1862–1952) had a varied career as actor, producer, novelist, journalist and playwright. Born in Louisiana, Kentucky, she moved to England in 1889 to become the foremost Ibsen actor and producer. She published several novels under the name of C. E. Raimond. Her first novel, *George Mandeville's Husband* (1894) is a satire on pseudo-intellectual women novelists. *The Magnetic North* (1904), set in Alaska, where she went to search for her brother, became a best-seller. Her novels include *The Open Door* (1898), concerned with heredity and the ethics of suicide, and *My Little Sister* (1913), which deals with the white slave trade. She was a member of the militant Women's Social and Political Union from 1906 to 1912. A founder of the Actresses' Franchise League, in 1908 she became the first president of the Women Writers' Suffrage League. The controversial play, *Alan's Wife*, written with Florence Bell, was followed by the play, *Votes for Women!* in 1907, written in the same year as she published *The Convert*, a novel version of the play. She gave the profits to suffrage organizations, and to help buy Backsetton Farm as a retreat for professional women. After the war she became an active member of the equal rights organization, the Six Point Group, and one of the founding directors of the journal, *Time and Tide*.

Olive Emilie Albertina Schreiner (1855–1920) was born on a mission farm at Wittebergen, Basutoland, to a German father and English mother, the ninth of their twelve children. She was a socialist feminist, associated with the Fellowship of the New Life, which she joined in 1881 when she moved to London, and the Women's League of the Social Democratic Foundation. Her membership of the Men and Women's Club chaired by Karl Pearson, led to close correspondence between them during 1886. She returned to South Africa in 1889 and married Samuel Cronwright, a farmer and politician who took the name Cronwright-Schreiner. She gave birth to a daughter who lived only a few hours in 1895; three miscarriages followed, and she had no other children. She wrote the novels, *The Story of an African Farm* (1883), *Trooper Peter Halkett of Mashonaland* (1897); and the short stories, *Dreams* (1890) and *Dream Life and Real Life* (1909); the polemic work, *Woman and Labour* (1911); and the novels *From Man to Man, Or Perhaps Only ...* (1926) and *Undine* (1929) were published posthumously. She died in South Africa in 1920.

Abbreviations

Brooke, Emma Frances
SW   *A Superfluous Woman* (London: William Heinemann, 1894)

Caird, Mona
DD   *The Daughters of Danaus* (1894) (New York: Feminist Press, 1989)
MM   *The Morality of Marriage and Other Essays on the Status and Destiny of Woman* (London: George Kedway, 1897)

Cross(e), Victoria (Annie Sophie Cory)
TWWD   *The Woman Who Didn't* (London: John Lane, 1895)
'Theodora' 'Theodora: A Fragment' (1895) in Elaine Showalter (ed.), *Daughters of Decadence: Women Writers of the Fin de Siècle* (London: Virago, 1993)
AL   *Anna Lombard* (1901) (London: John Long, 1902)

Dixon, Ella Hepworth
SMW   *The Story of a Modern Woman* (London: John Lane, 1895)

Grand, Sarah (Frances Elizabeth McFall)
THT   *The Heavenly Twins* (1893) (Michigan: Michigan University Press, 1992)
BB   *The Beth Book* (1897) Reprint of 1898 edn. (Bristol: Thoemmes Press, 1994)
'TU'   'The Undefinable: A Fantasia', *Emotional Moments* (1908) in Elaine Showalter (ed.), *Daughters of*

	Decadence: Feminist Fiction at the Fin de Siècle (London: Virago, 1993), 262–87
OMN	*Our Manifold Nature* (London: William Heinemann, 1894)

'Iota' (Caffyn, Katherine Mannington)

YA	*A Yellow Aster* (London: Hutchinson and Co., 1894)
CS	*A Comedy in Spasms* (London: Hutchinson and Co., 1895)

Lee, Vernon (Violet Paget)

'AD'	'Amour Dure', *Hauntings: Fantastic Stories* (London: William Heinemann, 1890). Victorian Women Writers Project Indiana University: http://www.indiana.edu/ ~ letrs/vwwp/lee/hauntings.html

Schreiner, Olive

AF	*The Story of an African Farm* (1883) (London: Penguin, 1995)
WL	*Woman And Labour* (1911) (London: Virago, 1988)

1

An Introduction to the New Woman

In Marie Corelli's hugely successful sensation novel of 1895, *The Sorrows of Satan*, one of the many attacks on modern literature is directed at writing by New Women. Advising a would-be author on how to catch the public's interest, a publisher tells him not to write 'a book on any positively indecent subject – that can be left to the "New" woman [one of those] self-degrading creatures who delineate their fictional heroines as wallowing in unchastity, and who write freely on subjects which men would hesitate to name'.[1] Flagrantly exhibitionist itself, *The Sorrows of Satan* is an advocate, through the person of the novelist Mavis Clare – 'that woman-wearer of the laurel-crown – that keeper of the lilies of purity and peace' – of old-fashioned values in which women's 'greatest right, their highest privilege, is to guide and guard the souls of men.'[2]

At the time Corelli was writing, the New Woman had become, or was becoming, notorious. A century later, after a long period of neglect, feminist history and criticism began to catch up with her, and attempts to define and characterize her have abounded. Part of her appeal, in both *fins de siècles*, seems to have been her elusiveness and her resistance to fixed categorization. Recent accounts have described her as 'a sociological phenomenon and a literary type [who] focused a number of contemporary debates concerning the emancipation of women, and joined them to a movement to modernize contemporary fiction through the exploration of the social constraints on feminine sexuality.'[3] Another writer has described her as a woman who 'tended to be a radical intellectual, who extended her feminism beyond the

1

claims of the organised women's movement for civil rights to the sphere of sexual ethics.'[4] Although both accounts emphasize sexuality, they indicate a division in modern thought concerning the New Woman: the first sees her as a fiction and an abstraction and the second as a historical reality. What most critics agree on, however, is that the feminism of New Women was not homogeneous but multiple. Feminism was (and is) not a unified voice but a diversity of ideological positions and platforms, making classification of texts a complex enterprise. Even if they shared identities – those largely of British, colonial, white, middle- and upper-class women – the formal and thematic concerns of the New Woman writers were diverse. Although clear ideological positions and identifications with certain political campaigns can be identified, the dynamics of their interaction with other literary movements and aesthetic agendas of the period do not allow a unified or consistent subjectivity to be posited for the New Woman writer. The professional networks and social circles in which women writers moved prove that one term does not need to be exclusive of another; literary fields were not so totally self-contained as to prevent writers from straddling them.

When Corelli attacked her in *The Sorrows of Satan*, the New Woman had been named two years earlier and Corelli was attacking a target already identified, confirming rather than forming prejudices. Although the label had been used as early as 1865 by the *Westminster Review* to describe the heroines of sensation fiction,[5] it seems to have gained an independent life in 1894, starting with an article entitled 'The New Woman' by the romantic novelist Ouida, in a reply to an article by Sarah Grand, 'The New Aspect of the Woman Question'.[6] Grand had written a scathing attack on men who were incapable of appreciating the qualities of emancipated women; 'the cow-woman and the scum-woman are well within [his] range . . . but the new woman is a little above him . . . sitting apart in silent contemplation . . . until at last she has solved the problem and proclaimed for herself what was wrong with Home-is-the-Woman's Sphere'.[7] Ouida introduced the important capital letters: 'in the English language there are conspicuous at the present time two words which designate two unmitigated bores . . . The Workingman and the Woman, the New Woman'. As Ellen Jordan has pointed out,[8] *Punch*, which had been peddling anti-feminist jokes for

2

some years, made the decisive link between the name, the supposed characteristics of this kind of woman, and that they were objects of derision and perhaps also of fear. In late May 1894 the following sketch appeared: 'The New Woman, "Ouida" says "the New Woman" is an unmitigated bore. "Sarah Grand" declares that man, morally, "is in his infancy" and that "now Woman holds out a strong hand to the Child-Man and insists on helping him" by "spanking proper principles into him in the nursery".

> There is a New Woman, and what do you think?
> She lives upon nothing but Foolscap and Ink!
> But though Foolscap and Ink are the whole of her diet,
> The nagging New Woman can never be quiet!'

Once *Punch* took hold of the name and the stereotype, 'it refused to release its grip; as late as 10 January 1900 it asked whether the New Woman was alive or dead'.[9]

Although the New Woman had been named in May 1894, she had been around for some years before that. Indeed, she was always part of the nineteenth-century 'woman question' as a figure to whom the rights and opportunities for women could not be satisfied by marriage or women's limited educational and employment prospects. The feminists of the middle years of the century, those doughty pioneers of the suffrage and educational reform movements,[10] were the progenitors of the New Woman. Some of them, like Jessie Boucherett, were still campaigning at the end of the century, joined by others of similar purpose, such as Helen Blackburn, editor of the *Englishwoman's Review*, and Emily Davies, who, aged 76, and after 50 years of continuous feminist activity, led a suffrage deputation to the Prime Minister in 1906.

By the 1880s some limited gains had been made: Girton College, Cambridge and Lady Margaret Hall and Somerville College, Oxford had been founded, and the Married Women's Property Act of 1870 had ensured that a woman's earnings after marriage remained her property.[11] But a woman's rights over her children were still insecure and she did not have access to divorce on equal terms with her husband. As far as the vote was concerned, there had also been some success, with women rate-payers, generally widows and single women, able to vote in

3

local elections. But this was not the case in parliamentary elections. The Reform Bill of 1884 had extended the franchise to almost all men but the Women's Suffrage amendment, which would have given a limited vote to women, was defeated, largely through William Gladstone's opposition. As Ray Strachey has argued,[12] this 'betrayal' by the Liberal Party, followed by similar betrayals in the years to come, bred deep distrust of party allegiances among suffragists and helped develop a more independent and eventually more militant suffrage movement. The ground for the emergence of the New Woman, and for her exposure in the media, was fertile.

The demands for the franchise and for access to higher education and the professions were, of course, middle class. Whether as a concept or as a reality, the New Woman herself for the most part was a middle-class phenomenon, and although much was written about her, she was a minority figure, with most women untouched by her presence or her ideas. The context in which she emerged was one of economic depression, which bore particularly severely on the working classes. The end of the 1870s saw widespread unemployment and the increase in an underclass of the chronically poor and long-term unemployed. H. M. Hyndman, in his essay 'English Workers as They Are', described 'a certain percentage' of these as 'beyond hope of being reached at all. Crushed down into the gutter, physically and mentally by their social surroundings, they can but die out, leaving, it is hoped, no progeny as a burden on a better state of things.'[13] It would become a matter of concern to some New Women that the hopeless poor refused to die out but instead continued to produce numerous burdensome progeny.

By the end of the century there were, according to the 1891 census, nearly 2.5 million unmarried women, 900,000 more than unmarried men.[14] These surplus or 'redundant' women had been an anxiety since the middle years of the century, and would continue so up to and during the inter-war years. It was apparent that something must be done about them and wage-earning independence was a solution that appealed to women's rights campaigners and a fair number of others too. This is the theme of George Gissing's *The Odd Women* (1893) in which five women attempt to earn a living, with depressing results. Gissing's many targets in the novel include the institution of

4

marriage, the 'separate spheres' which trap women and men in stereotypical gender roles, and the notion of romantic love peddled by novelists: 'What is more vulgar than the ideal of novelists?' Rhoda Nunn asks. 'There is the sexual instinct, of course, but that is quite a different thing; the novelists won't talk about that . . . The paltry creatures daren't tell the one truth that would be profitable. The result is that women imagine themselves noble and glorious when they are most near the animals' (Ch. 6). Rhoda Nunn is a New Woman herself in that she runs a business, refuses to marry an unsatisfactory suitor whom she nevertheless loves, and, as her name suggests, holds to an ideal of independence and integrity. But to some extent she is pathologized as frigid and neurotic and the outcome for women, as presaged by her, is uncompromising; her closing words on seeing a baby girl are 'Poor little child!'

Many historians have pointed out that the myth of the Victorian woman as home-bound has overlooked the fact that from the 1850s[15] onwards over a quarter of all girls and women over the age of ten were employed, comprising 30 per cent of the whole labour force. Although by the 1890s employment for middle-class women had increased,[16] the vast majority of employed women were manual workers. The most numerous of these were domestic servants. The rising wealth of the middle classes had resulted overall in a 50 per cent increase in domestic servants in the period from the 1850s to the 1870s. Although this increase declined in the years to the end of the century, it remained a 'compulsive influence on the female labour force',[17] offering as it did to take girls as young as twelve into service with the promise of good training and secure employment. This may have been fulfilled in some cases but many servants were overworked and exploited, with wages as low as £10 a year for a general maid. The average annual wage in 1899 for female domestic servants was £17/16s. in London, £15/10s. outside London.[18] Numerically, the so-called 'sweated trades' came next, whether in small workshops or increasingly in factories towards the end of the century. Textile and agricultural workers and a whole range of occupations such as straw-plaiters, shop keepers, milliners, shoe-makers and glovers contributed to a vast population of working-class women to whom the New Woman would be unknown and whose concerns they would have regarded as irrelevant to their lives. As David Rubinstein says, 'Exploited by their husbands, by their employers, by society at large, most working-class women were in no position to rebel against social injustice.'[19]

To some women, however, this unregulated, suffering and volatile mass of workers presented an opportunity to develop traditional Victorian charitable activities into a profession, or at least into a full-time commitment. Beatrice Potter (later Beatrice Webb) wrote of the years between 1883, when she began research into living conditions in the East End of London, and 1887 which saw the publication of her contribution to Charles Booth's *The Life and Labour of the People in London*, that they were 'the crucial years of my life . . . From being a lively and, at times, good-looking society girl, assumed to be ready to follow her elder sisters' example in making a happy and otherwise satisfactory marriage, I was transformed into, I will not say a professional, but a professed brain-worker, overtly out for a career of my own.'[20]

Although Beatrice Webb is not usually classed as such, her discontents and ambitions were typical of the New Woman, as was her determination to live by her own standards and desires. Very much in love with Joseph Chamberlain, she could not accept his demands for a wife who would be uncritically devoted to his aims and give him 'uncompromising admiration'. Her sense of the conflict in her nature was one shared by many women, and will become a dominant theme in the fiction of the period: 'Alas! For we poor women! Even our strong minds do not save us from tender feelings . . . [T]his hopeless independence of thought that makes my mind so distasteful to many people; and rightly so, for a woman *should* be more or less dependent and receptive. However, I must perforce go through the world with my mind as it is – and *be true to myself*.'[21]

If Beatrice Potter is not generally seen as a New Woman, if she illustrates that difficulty in fitting the concept to an actual person, who did fit the concept? In *Punch's* brief skit, the stereotypical lineaments of the New Woman start to appear. She was vocal and a writer, she was persistent in asserting her equality with if not her superiority to men, she was ascetic in life-style, unfeminine in manner, and highly moralistic. But as Sally Ledger has said, 'the New Woman as a concept was, from its inception, riddled with contradictions.'[22] On the one hand she was highly moralistic, on the other she was characterized by sexual licence, an outrageous lifestyle and a repudiation of heterosexual norms, including marriage, although, as will become clear, motherhood would become a crusading concern for her. She was also frequently idealistic about the possibility of a superior union with the opposite sex. This last characteristic did not, however, prevent her from being perceived as an advocate of free love, a scourge of conventional marriage, and neglectful of her children. She was also likely to smoke, swear, ride a bicycle, wear 'rational' dress, and generally behave in a manly fashion.[23]

> She flouts Love's caresses
> Reforms ladies' dresses
> And scorns the Man-Monster's tirade;
> She seems scarcely human
> This mannish New Woman
> This Queen of the Blushless Brigade.'[24]

She was descended from women and girls similarly labelled for improper behaviour: 'the Girl of the Period' of the 1860s, the Wild Women of the very early 1890s.[25]

But actual women who fit the stereotype are not easy to find. There were many women engaged in feminist activities who would probably not have accepted the name New Woman. These included, for example, women living unconventional lives, like Michael Field (pseudonym for aunt and niece), Isadora Duncan, or Eleanor Marx, and there were women who took up unconventional occupations or pastimes, like the women who took to smoking or to cycling in rational dress. There were the women journalists who wrote for or edited feminist or avant-garde periodicals of the time, such as Lydia Becker who edited the *Women's Suffrage Journal* from 1870 to 1890, Lady Henry Somerset, who edited the *Woman's Signal, A Weekly Record of the Progress of the Woman's Movement*, or Ella D'Arcy, who helped to edit the *Yellow Book* (1894–7). One of the most interesting of the periodicals of the time was the liberal-feminist *Shafts, A Paper for Women and the Working Classes* (1892–9); its first editor, Margaret Sibthorp, was particularly keen to review New Woman fiction (she reviewed Sarah Grand's *The Heavenly Twins*, for example) and also to promote frank and accurate discussion about sexual

7

relations. Women writing at this time on feminist issues were various, ranging from the birth-control advocate Annie Besant, who published *Marriage, As It Was, As It Is, and As It Should Be: A Plea for Reform*, in 1882, to the initially more 'respectable' Emmeline Pethick-Lawrence, who founded and wrote about working girls' clubs in the 1890s. She later became a suffragette, joining the Pankhursts' Women's Suffrage and Political Union in 1906, the year of the first of her six imprisonments for suffragette activities. There were women like Maria Sharpe who, along with Eleanor Marx and Olive Schreiner, belonged to avant-garde groups such as Karl Pearson's Men and Women's Club; and there were those involved in campaign politics, like the trade unionists Margaret Bondfield and Clementina Black. There were also the pioneer professional women, particularly those in medicine. The example of Dr Mary Murdoch is instructive; she qualified as a doctor in the early 1890s, rode a bicycle, then drove a pony trap, and finally a car in the early years of the twentieth century. She passionately supported the suffrage campaigns, and 'at no time would she have thought that marriage offered compensation for the barter of her personal freedom'.[26] And yet possessing all these attributes of a New Woman, she neither considered herself to be one, nor did others. There was something else required of a woman before she could be described as New. In fact, the New Woman was something of a chimera: no-one and every-one, a figure of speech almost, which could be invoked and appropriated to represent what was subversive and modern in female behaviour.

Whatever she was, the New Woman was, of course, part of an obsession with newness. In *The Eighteen Nineties*, published in 1913, Holbrook Jackson looked back on a decade he had lived through in which 'the adjective "new" ... was applied ... to indicate extreme modernity'. He listed its usage: the New Paganism, the New Voluptuousness, the New Spirit, the New Realism, the New Hedonism, the New Fiction and the New Woman. There was also newness in journalism, particularly the *New Age*, 'a penny weekly with a humanitarian and radical objective', followed shortly by W. E. Henley's the *New Review*.[27] As Elaine Showalter has shown, the end of a century tends 'not only to suggest but intensify crises' and a sense of collapse, change and rebirth. The term *fin-de-siècle* originated in France in the 1880s and spread rapidly throughout Europe. It was, she suggests, 'weighted with symbolic and historical meaning' which invoked anarchy, particularly sexual anarchy. 'During this period "feminism" and "homosexuality" first came into use as New Women and male aesthetes redefined the meanings of femininity and masculinity.'[28]

As Showalter suggests, it was an attempt to redefine femininity and the female that marked out the New Woman from her feminist sisters who worked to change the legal, educational and employment status of women but who were on the whole content with their female natures, including their sexual natures. They did not wish to attack the basis on which the relations between the sexes rested. But at least as a concept, this was what the New Woman wished to do. If there was any common ground between the women who register most resonantly as New Woman writers, it was an insistence on the need to explore, redefine and celebrate women's sexuality, and a need to show how artificially women's sexual nature had been constructed (and contaminated) by a male-dominated society. Sarah Grand, George Egerton, Mona Caird, Victoria Cross – these and other recognizably New Women differed in political and aesthetic concerns but they came together over this question of women's sexuality and the related question of the relation between men and women.

Most commentators agree that before she was named, the New Woman made her first utterance in Olive Schreiner's *The Story of an African Farm*.[29] Appearing under the pseudonym of Ralph Iron, this novel, published in 1883, was an immediate commercial success. Its heroine, Lyndall, one of two orphans on a Boer farm, was recognized as a new voice of protest against the conditions and conditioning of a woman's life. Chapter 4 of the second part of the novel is an extended feminist outcry:

'Look at this little chin of mine, Waldo, with the dimple in it. It is but a small part of my person; but though I had a knowledge of all things under the sun, and the wisdom to use it, and the deep loving heart of an angel, it would not stead me through life like this little chin. I can win money with it, I can win love; I can win power with it, I can win fame ... A little weeping, a little wheedling, a little self-degradation, a little careful use of our advantages, and then some man will say – "Come, be my wife!" ... When we ask to be doctors, lawyers, law-makers, anything but ill-paid drudges, they say, – No; but you have men's chivalrous attention; now think of that and be satisfied! What would you do without it?   (*AF* 188–90)

Lyndall's protest looks back to Mary Wollstonecraft's *Vindication of the Rights of Women* (1792) in its insistence on an education for women other than the ability 'to cook a dinner or dress herself well', and on the necessity for women as mothers – 'that one great and noble work left to them' – to be cultured and rational. It also looks forward to Simone de Beauvoir's *The Second Sex* (1949) in its analysis of the conditioning that results in women's subordination and in their bad faith in accepting that subordination: 'They begin to shape us to our cursed end when we are tiny things . . . Then the curse begins to act on us. It finishes its work when we are grown women, who no more look out wistfully at a more healthy life; we are contented. We fit our sphere as a Chinese woman's foot fits her shoe' (*AF* 189). In this image of the footbinding of girls and women, Lyndall's speech echoes that of a frustrated woman nearer to her in time than Wollstonecraft or de Beauvoir. Florence Nightingale's turbulent *Cassandra*, written in 1852, compared the 'form that Chinese feet assume when denied their proper development' to the stunted lives of women: 'Why have women passion, intellect, moral activity – these three – and a place in society where no one of the three can be exercised?' To Cassandra/Nightingale, 'It seems as if the female spirit of the world were mourning everlastingly over blessings, not *lost*, but which she has never had, and which in her discouragement she feels that she will never have, they are so far off.'[30] Though the essay was privately printed in 1859, Cassandra's protest was not publicly heard for more than half a century, until the 'fragment', as Ray Strachey calls it, was published as an appendix to *The Cause* (1928), her account of the women's movement in Britain.

In spite of her passionate protest, Nightingale was never at ease with the suffrage campaigns, and she would not have been willing to be classified as a New Woman. But she did not sign the anti-suffrage petition organized in 1889 by Mrs Humphry Ward, who became the first president, in 1908, of the Anti-Suffrage League. A hundred and four women, mostly wives of politicians and men of letters, but also nurses and novelists, signed 'An Appeal Against Female Suffrage'. The 'Appeal' based its objection to extending the suffrage to women on biological essentialism. Women are and should be debarred from the strenuousness of public life, whether in politics, business or the armed forces, by 'the disabilities of sex, or by strong formations of custom and habit resting ultimately upon physical difference, against which it is useless to contend'. They should exert influence through the exercise of their 'natural position and functions which might be seriously impaired by their admission to the turmoil of active political life'. If they were to enter the struggle, 'their natural eagerness and quickness of temper would probably make them hotter partisans than men'. A mere outward equality with men, such as the vote would allow, would be 'not only vain but demoralising [and] a total misconception of woman's true dignity and special mission'.[31]

The familiar and enduring arguments that women would be harmed by full entry into political life, that they would be emotional if not hysterical in carrying out public duties, and that they had better stay at home and exercise influence over men, were, of course, the very arguments that the suffragists and the New Woman disputed. But they did not necessarily dispute the notion of biological difference. The suffrage leader Millicent Garrett Fawcett wrote in her reply to Mrs Ward's 'Appeal' that 'we neither deny nor minimize the differences between men and women'.[32] Nor did either group reject the idea of women's moral influence, in the case of writers like George Egerton or Sarah Grand believing women to be morally superior to men. To bracket suffragists and New Women together is, however, to simplify a complex alignment. As Constance Rover has pointed out, 'the women's emancipation movement in England ... was dominated by that sense of propriety and respectability which was the hallmark of the middle classes during that period'. Sally Ledger confirms this: 'the mainstream women's movement of the nineteenth century steered well clear of the sexual libertarians, preferring to focus on civic and constitutional issues rather than on the potentially more disreputable debates surrounding gender and sexuality.'[33] Rover notes that Ray Strachey's classic history of the women's movement, *The Cause*, celebrates Josephine Butler as a heroine of the women's movement for her campaign for the repeal of the Contagious Diseases Acts, whereas Annie Besant, pioneer of the birth control movement, is not mentioned.[34] If shunning the birth control movement was one result of this respectability, suspicion of the New Woman, with her alleged outspokenness about sexual behaviour and her sometime advocacy of free love, was another. Millicent Garrett Fawcett, for example, in her review of Grant Allen's novel *The Woman who Did* (1895), wrote that such as he was no friend of the women's movement because he links together 'the claim of women to citizenship and social and industrial independence with attacks upon marriage and the family'.[35] Equally, some New Women were dismissive of the suffrage movement. George Egerton, for example, had no interest in the vote, nor in trying to extend and equalize women's employment opportunities. 'Her position was that she wanted "not civil but *sexual* rights for women".'[36]

The attitude of New Women to marriage was complex and ambivalent. Very few of them repudiated it altogether. The commonest approach was that it should be reformed, not replaced. Sarah Grand, for example, although highly critical of bourgeois marriage, especially its double standards of sexual morality, nevertheless had in her sights the kind of marriage that Tennyson's poem, *The Princess*, published as early as 1847, advocated:

> Self-reverent each and reverencing each,
> Distinct in individualities . . .
> Then reign the world's great bridals, chaste and calm:
> Then springs the crowning race of humankind'
>
> (Bk. 7, 274–9)

At the end of Grand's *The Beth Book* (1897), after a disastrous marriage to a bullying doctor, who is implicated in the Lock hospitals where women were examined under the Contagious Diseases Acts, and who is also a vivisectionist, Beth sees a New Man approaching on horseback across the fields and is reminded of Lancelot in 'The Lady of Shalott': ' "'A bowshot from her bower-eaves, / He rode between the barley-sheaves." ' . . . It seemed as if she ought to have known it from the first, known that he would come like that at last, that he had been coming, coming, coming through all the years' (*BB* 527). Even Mona Caird, whose essay 'Marriage' in the *Daily Telegraph* in 1888 placed no reliance on romantic idealism to reform marriage, was a reformer rather than an abolitionist. She reminded her readers that the institution was relatively recent, that 'the careless use of words' about human nature 'and especially "woman's nature" ' obscured rational thought about the 'vexatious failure' of modern marriage, which must be rescued from a mercenary society and 'torn from the arms of "Respectability" '. Once that had been achieved, an ideal, perhaps a 'Utopian impossibility', and certainly one influenced by John Stuart Mill's *On the Subjection of Women* (1869), could be realized in which marriage would be free, with 'the economic independence of woman [as] the first condition of free marriage'.[37] The public response to Caird's *Telegraph* essay was remarkably indicative of the sensitivity of the topic at this time; 27,000 letters poured into the newspaper. As Judith R. Walkowitz has noted, the newspaper, with perhaps unconscious irony, printed many of the letters on the left-hand side of the news-sheet whilst on the right-hand side were accounts of the acts of Jack the Ripper. This was a time of heightened discourses about sexuality: in Walkowitz's words, the late Victorian world saw a 'conjunction of shifting sexual practices, sexual scandals and political mobilizations' which provided the historical conditions for the elaboration of narratives of sexual danger. She argues that, along with the Ripper murders, W. T. Stead's 'The Maiden Tribute of Modern Babylon' in the *Pall Mall Gazette* in 1885 (the same year as the Labouchère amendment to the Criminal Law Amendment Act criminalized male homosexuality), with its sensational exposure of the trade in child prostitutes, were major factors in propelling the debates on sexuality into public view.[38] New Women were vociferous participants in this debate, particularly as moral reformers.

The desire of New Women to reform marriage and introduce a new sexual morality related to an end-of-century fear of venereal disease and its consequence in the birth of enfeebled children. Women's sexual health was at stake, and also their maternal capabilities. Behind these anxieties lay the threat of degeneration, affecting the health of the whole nation and its ability to sustain an empire. Syphilis in particular had become a sensational issue by the end of the century, and was to be annexed by the suffrage movement in Christabel Pankhurst's notorious pamphlet, 'Plain Facts about a Great Evil' (1913), written in the wake of a petition by doctors for a Royal Commission 'to enquire into the subject of venereal disease'. Pankhurst's diagnosis was that 'the cause of sexual disease is the subjection of women' and her recommended cure was 'Votes for women and chastity for men.' New Woman novels prepare the ground for this with their many references to syphilis, as will be discussed in more detail in Chapter 2. Sarah Grand's *The Heavenly Twins* (1893) gives the most graphic indictment of a double standard that sanctions contamination of women and children by men's sexual excess. Bram Stoker's *Dracula* (1897) also resonates with references to syphilis; the vampires' activities are always of a sexual nature, and their victims inherit the disease through an exchange of fluids. Mina Harker is somewhat of a New Woman in her independence and also in her support for a New Man who will cleanse the world (particularly England) of sexually unclean creatures and become a fitting husband and the father of her children.

The ideas of evolutionary science saturate the cultural narratives of the turn of the century, creating newly secularized explanations for socio-economic formations and the disciplining of gendered subjectivities. Charles Darwin's *On the Origin of Species by Means of Natural Selection* (1859) set out his revolutionary theory of evolution; its tenet of the natural selection of chance mutations challenged Victorian society's deep-rooted belief in divine providence and the fixity of the species. Whilst he did not address human social evolution in any depth in *The Origin of Species*, Darwin returned to his theory of sexual selection and its implications for the relations between men and women in *The Descent of Man* in 1871. Subsequent discoveries in biology in the 1880s and debates over hereditarian paradigms compounded new understandings of the self, memory and will in the domain of evolutionary psychology, and are embedded in writers' narratives, from the detective fiction of Arthur Conan Doyle to the realism of Thomas Hardy, from the polemicism of Brooke to the aestheticism of Emma Brooke and Mona Caird.

The context to much New Woman writing on sexuality and maternity was the late nineteenth-century eugenics debate. The term 'eugenics' was coined by Francis Galton, Darwin's cousin, in 1883 and defined as 'the science of improving stock'. 'The improvement of our stock seems to me one of the highest objects that we can reasonably attempt.'[39] As Angelique Richardson has argued, this was an important departure from the idea that children were born 'naturally', by God's will: 'The idea that humans might breed selectively, that they might exercise control over the biological quality of the race, was given precise formulation and a new, apparently scientific, authority.'[40] Several New Women were central to the debate, particularly Sarah Grand, George Egerton, Emma Brooke and Mona Caird, offering a spectrum of differing positions on the question. Angelique Richardson suggests that Grand and Egerton combined their commitment to feminism 'with a belief in biological determinism and eugenics; while Caird adopted a radically different position, arguing for the historically rather than the biologically determined nature of social evolution, and sought to reveal the social biases that made up and motivated biological discourse.'[41] Whether a man is a fit breeding partner, and even whether an 'unfit' child should survive, are questions that exercise New Woman's writing; Grand's *The Beth Book* is an attack on degeneracy, Beth's husband having the defective teeth of a syphilitic and the high colour of a consumptive. He dies, appropriately, of 'fatty degeneration', leaving Beth fortunately childless. Egerton was even more vehemently eugenic, writing that 'it is no woman's part in life to play the *role* of relieving officers for the preservation of wastrels ... any more than it is her duty to go on mothering children to an inheritance of disease or insanity'.[42] She was a fierce advocate of the power of the maternal urge, and many of her stories dwell on this, as in 'The Heart of the Apple' in which the heroine is 'a genetic creature, fashioned of the right ground-stuff for the renewal of life'. If this urge is best fulfilled by mating outside of marriage, so be it. Mona Caird's fierce criticism of the rise of biological determinism, particularly in its aspect of negative eugenics which aimed at eliminating 'inferior' stock, sought to protect the rights of the individual. In a speech of 1913, quoted by Richardson, Caird expressed her dismay at the direction eugenicist ideas were taking: 'Is it quite impossible to awaken the public to the awful and innumerable dangers which confront us all, as soon as the protection of personal rights is withdrawn? ... Can we not

15

persuade our contemporaries to ask themselves if, for instance, the apostles of eugenics have shrunk from any measure, however outrageous, which they thought promised the desired results? Provided the end is gained, the individual must pay the price.'[43]

Part of the eugenicist agenda was what was felt to be an imperialist obligation. Between 1870 and 1900 the British Empire was extended by 4.75 million square miles, increasing the number of British subjects by some 88 million. To many eugenicists, the white European, particularly the English, represented the culmination of human development. Other races were inferior, Karl Pearson arguing, for example, that the Kaffir and the Negro were 'bad stock': 'Educate them and nurture them as you will, I do not believe that you will succeed in modifying the stock.'[44] English men and women owed it to their race to breed physically and mentally fit individuals selectively, to maintain the strength of the British themselves and to administer the Empire. Powerful threats to this scientific approach to national well-being came from contamination abroad – 'intercrossing', as Pearson calls it, which may raise the bad stock but then 'the good is lowered' – and degeneracy at home. Degeneracy, interpreted for Pearson, Galton and others by Max Nordau in *Degeneration* (1895) as 'a morbid deviation from the normal form', meant effeminacy, emotionalism, hysteria, aestheticism and general unmanliness in men, implying, of course, homosexuality. A further abnormality was the stunted growth and undeveloped intellect of the crushed and hopeless poor of Hyndman's description. 'A weird and uncanny people', as C. F. G. Masterman described them: 'They have poured in as dense black masses from the eastern railways; they have streamed across the bridges from the marshes and desolate places across the river ... emerging like rats from a drain, blinking in the sunshine.'[45]

Throughout the discourse on sexual health and the future of the race ran this awareness of England's own 'Dark Continent'. The East End of London was an unknown land equal in its terrors to those of Africa. New Woman fiction came into full prominence at the same time as writing on this aspect of English life reached maturity. From William Booth's *In Darkest England and the Way Out* (1890) to Masterman's *From the Abyss* (1902), the *fin de siècle* abounds with sociological and anthropological enquiries into the conditions of the destitute and criminal sections of society. Working-class and destitute women and their sexual health are, however, notably missing from New Woman writings, which are predominantly middle-class in orientation. A possible exception to this was Margaret Harkness, second cousin of Beatrice Webb, a parson's daughter who left home to work with the Salvation Army, and joined the Social Democratic Federation but was disillusioned with it within a few months. Gerd Bjørhovde includes Harkness's writings amongst the 're-bellious structures' of New Woman fiction but her *A City Girl* (1887) and *A Manchester Shirtmaker* (1890) feature female protag-onists whose New Woman characteristics are more to do with collectivist protest against harsh employment conditions than sexual individualism. As Bjørhovde has suggested, in Harkness's novels, 'working-class individual[s] can do nothing; but together they may achieve power to do all sorts of things'.[46] Otherwise, as Ann Heilmann has argued, 'It is a striking feature of the feminist fiction of the time that social hierarchies remain largely unchallenged by the very women (authors and characters) who struggle so hard to overcome sexual inequalities.'[47]

There were women active in the emerging socialist groupings in the 1880s and 1890s, like Isobella Ford, whose New Woman novel *On the Threshold* (1895) suggested a connection between feminism and socialism, and Eleanor Marx, whose article written with Edward Aveling on 'The Woman Question from a Socialist Point of View'[48] argued that the only way in which women's cause could be advanced and the married state improved was through a socialist reform of society. Eleanor Marx would not have described herself as a New Woman. The distance most New Women maintained from politics and their individualist and apparently elitist concerns conspired to isolate them from women activists, just as their perceived sexual deviance alien-ated them from the respectable classes.

For although, as we have seen, New Women disapproved of effeminacy in men, they were themselves often associated with male Decadents or Aesthetes, and, by extension, with homosex-uals. The New Woman and the Aesthete were frequently linked in the periodical press as sexual degenerates, because both challenged conventional constructions of femininity and mascu-linity, and both tended to promote more candid discussions of sex and sexuality. Many New Women disparaged the identification made between themselves and the male aesthetes, and indeed, there was little shared ideological ground between them, except the willingness to discuss sexual relations more openly than before. As Sally Ledger has pointed out, 'the perceived connection between the New Woman and decadence ... meant that the fate of the New Woman was inextricably linked to the public disgracing of Oscar Wilde'[49] in May 1895 when Wilde was sentenced to two years imprisonment with hard labour for committing acts of 'gross indecency'. In December 1895, *Punch* announced 'THE END OF THE NEW WOMAN – The crash has come at last.' And reviewing Hardy's *Jude the Obscure* in February 1896, H. G. Wells was eager to announce that 'it is now the better part of a year since the collapse of the "New Woman" fiction began'.[50]

Though such pronouncements were premature, certainly as far as the drama was concerned, there was a sense that the time of New Woman writing was drawing to a close. A new, militant phase of feminism was soon to begin and the emphasis in women's writing would fall more explicitly on suffrage; an example is Gertrude Colmore's *Suffragette Sally* (1911), or in opposition to it, Mrs Humphry Ward's *Delia Blanchflower* (1915). In its heyday, New Woman fiction had certainly appealed to readers. Sarah Grand's *The Heavenly Twins*, for example, was reprinted six times in its first year of publication, and, as Kate Flint points out, the image of women reading this novel became a New Woman cliché.[51] To that doughty opponent of the New Woman in all her manifestations, Hugh Stutfield, in 'The Psychology of Feminism', in *Blackwood's Magazine* in 1897, this appeal signalled a morbid imagination and degeneracy of taste amongst its female readers.[52]

For the Edwardians, New Women and their writing represented an important development. To Elizabeth Robins, who would become one of the most active of suffragists, New Women blazed a trail, demonstrating that women writers need no longer play 'the sedulous ape', imitating men in both style and content.[53] They broke down barriers, particularly sexual barriers, about what could be written and they did so from woman's point of view, exploring, as George Egerton said, the *terra incognita* of a woman's mind and feelings. Moreover, as will become apparent, in doing so some of them, Egerton in particular, developed a style and form to counterbalance the prevailing realist mode. The short story, a modern form in the 1880s and 1890s, was well suited to her desire to write 'a little book ... merely to strike a few notes on the phases of the female character I knew to exist'.[54] A story like 'A Cross Line' (1893)[55] is not only broodingly evocative of female desire but is organized as a series of intensely realized psychological and emotional moments, without narrative linearity or closure. Its stylistic modernism looks forward to Mansfield and Woolf. Novelty of form, as well as content, is a distinguishing feature of New Woman fiction. As Kate Flint has argued:

> Its plotting is rarely complex in the sense of involving the reader in concealment and suspense; it is not predicated upon the reading process gratifying a desire for clarification and resolution. Its preferred form is the *Bildungsroman* ... Frequently it privileges childhood, both as a nostalgic realm which cannot be recaptured, and as a recognized site of gendered injustices. More noticeably, it presents a woman's life as process ... The employment of the *Bildungsroman* as a mode of narration encourages sympathetic identification on the reader's part ... Such fiction simultaneously invites intimacy, particularly through its incorporation of telling details ... and, in its adherence for the most part to realist principles, it claims typicality.[56]

But as will become clear, it was not only in the novel and the short story that the New Woman made her mark. New Woman drama, as we discuss in Chapter 4, was also innovative and subversive. Perhaps even more so, the non-fiction writing of women who, however loosely, can be described as New, was instrumental in bringing change in women's domestic and economic conditions. To take examples from a few years in the 1890s illustrates the range of writing by and about women and exposes the overlaps and slippages between socialist, trade union, feminist, misogynist, eugenicist and aesthetic positions and discourses during these turbulent years. Alice Zimmern, for example, published *The Renaissance of Girls' Education in England: A Record of Fifty Years' Progress* in 1898, Emma Brooke published 'The Position of Women: its Origin and History' in 1894 in *The Woman's Signal*, Mona Caird's collection of essays *The Morality of Marriage, and Other Essays* appeared in 1897, and Jane Hume

19

Clapperton was publishing her articles on domestic conditions in *Shafts*, including 'Reform in Domestic Life, as Required by Scientific Sociology' in 1893. These were in the same decade that saw the publication of Thomas Hardy's *Jude the Obscure* (1895), Grant Allen's *The Woman Who Did* (1895), Sarah Grand's *The Heavenly Twins* (1893), George Egerton's utopian communitarian short story 'The Regeneration of Two' (1894) and Mary Cholmondeley's *Red Pottage* (1899). As will be argued in the following chapters, 'The New Woman' was a label and an idea that moved across and through all these cultural products, pervasive if insubstantial, powerful if elusive.

2

Gender, Literary Value and the Woman of Genius

This chapter examines the ways in which the value and criticism of literary work in late nineteenth-century England was related to gender. The question of cultural production and consumption in the late nineteenth-century literary market was often constructed by its contemporary commentators to reflect the health of the nation, voicing anxieties about the consuming and consumed bodies of an imperial Britain in decline. The canons of cultural legitimacy were being reappraised, with 'realism' and 'romance' undergoing a process of redefinition that contested the association of gender with genre, and their respective forms of cultural capital or literary value. Female reformers redefining what literature might be, sought to negotiate the conflict between 'art for art's sake' (with its origins in a reactionary Romanticism) and the politics of the 'purpose novel' (with its 'new' ethical impulse). As a vehicle for feminist beliefs the novel must also be a formal intervention into masculine narratives and values; the authors of New Woman fiction aimed to expose the impurity of male sexuality, the sexual double standards and hypocrisy of marriage through their plots.[1] Yet their critics in the periodical press attacked 'the woman novel' as the source of contamination, and denounced such writing by both men and women as unwholesome and symptomatic of degeneration. The second part of the chapter will focus on women's representations of the woman artist in the modern city; the question of female 'genius' in relation to the difference between life and art for feminism involves contextualizing writers' perspectives on aesthetics and the role of literature within hierarchies of 'high' and 'low' art.

21

Recent New Woman fiction scholarship has defined the New Woman writers' goal as polemic; Ann Heilmann has argued that they were 'primarily concerned with getting their feminist politics across' through 'direct, immediate and unequivocal appeal' to a feminist agenda.[2] Rita Kranidis defines New Woman fiction as characterized by a political force in opposition to that of the cultural conservatism of aesthetic ideology;[3] a less bifurcated view recognizes both the political intent and the negotiation with aesthetic literary values which this fiction enacts. There was a dialogical relationship between New Woman writers and the other movements in the literary market; we will see how feminist discourse was not always strictly opposed to the techniques or values of this ideology. As well as the aim of communicating feminist ideas and politicizing readers, writers like Mona Caird, Victoria Cross and Sarah Grand were always engaged with stylistic and aesthetic considerations, not only polemical ends.

The perceived feminization of literature by cultural commentators who saw women and the 'woman question' as invading and corrupting the literary market involved an association between 'woman', the masses and 'low' culture. The New Woman fiction's success in the marketplace, with its political issues and polemical presentation of feminist concerns, was read as symptomatic of a cultural degeneration because it threatened masculinized 'high' art, a realm which should properly concern itself with abstract and universal questions. Andreas Huyssen argues that it is 'striking to observe how the political, psychological and aesthetic discourse around the turn of the century consistently and obsessively genders mass culture and the masses as feminine, while high culture, whether traditional or modern, clearly remains the privileged realm of male activities'.[4] He invites us to read this association as a projection of fear of losing power on a personal and political level, and as a threat to stable identity boundaries, of the male bourgeoisie.[5]

The prevailing cultural equation of an inauthentic mass culture with woman can be identified in biographer, poet and essayist Edmund Gosse's denunciation of the impacts of New Woman novel writers. In 'The Decay of Literary Taste' (1895)[6] Gosse decried what he saw as the demands of the new generation of readers, 'the vast, coarse, insatiable public',[7] in determining the production of the quality and form of literature – more novels. This reading public is characterized by traits popularly considered to be feminine: it is childlike in its 'incessant demand to be "told a story"' and it is irrational and excited by the new and the sensational to the point of hysteria and madness in its 'withdrawal of self-restraint'. This popular discourse of degeneration pathologizes both the producers and consumers of a popular, contemporary culture in which 'the intellectual signs of the times point to a sort of rising neurosis'.[8] Sounding Nordau's keynote in *Degeneration*, social, cultural and sexual deviance are drawn together through the figure of the feminist/hysteric. For Gosse, the older generation of patriarchs to which he belongs, the male gatekeepers of the literary canon and the rational, bourgeois order are threatened with being engulfed by a chaotic femininity: 'the door has been flung open, and the young men and women (especially the young women) are rushing in crowds'.[9]

Although the protest novel was, in popular cultural perception, associated with female consumers and producers, it was a popular mode for male and female writers alike. For example, despite his interest in and sympathies with the woman movement, and theirs with him, Thomas Hardy had attempted to distance his novel *Jude the Obscure* (1895) from being situated in the field of New Woman fiction; he expressed distaste at being classified with the popular or 'entrepreneurial' text derided as feminine, as if his text would be tainted by the more didactic flavour of these 'mass' products.[10] However, the popular science and fiction writer Grant Allen, capitalized on the topicality and popularity of New Woman fiction and adapted this trope to his own ends as an anti-feminist. Published in John Lane's *Keynote Series* with a number of writers also associated with Lane and Harland's *Yellow Book*, Allen's more radical fictions, *The Woman Who Did* (1895),[11] *The British Barbarians* (1895) and *A Splendid Sin* (1896), drew on the space created for franker discussion of sexual issues achieved by his contemporaries. Allen divided his fiction between the 'pot-boilers' of the field of mass-market literature, and his novels with a purpose, subtitled 'Hill-top Novels' – including *Philistia* (1884), *The British Barbarians*,[12] and *The Woman Who Did* – through which he aimed to reach impressionable female consumers, for, he stated: '[w]omen, in particular, are the chief readers of fiction, and it is women whom one mainly desires to arouse to interest in profound problems by the aid of this vehicle' (*British Barbarians* 13).

The effect of censorship on the novel was debated in the press in the 1880s and early 1890s in a number of public forums. Contributors deplored the stranglehold that the monopolist circulating libraries such as Edward Mudie and W. H. Smith exerted on the publishing industry. Such censorship rendered the novel suitable for the 'Young Person' or the 'British Matron' in the mythic personage of Mrs Grundy representing middle-class morality, and was determining the conventions of nineteenth-century literary realism. George Moore in his pamphlet *Literature at Nurse, or, Circulating Morals* (1885) had attacked the strictures of the circulating libraries in creating an emasculated literature.[13] An infamous opponent of the New Woman, Mrs Eliza Lynn Linton, endorsed the traditional domestic roles for middle-class women in 1868 in her controversial 'The Girl of the Period'; a series of articles on 'Wild Women' in the *Nineteenth Century* in the 1890s and elsewhere, continued her hostility to female emancipation. However, like some of her New Woman opponents, Linton's diatribe in 'Candour in English Fiction' in the *New Review* in 1890, demanded a greater realism and frankness in literary treatment of sexual relations – 'uncertificated love' – to reverse a decline in cultural values. Linton blames not the circulating libraries for the restrictions of the domestic romance genre, but the bourgeois morality of Mrs Grundy. The 'British Matron' she claims 'is the true censor of the Press, and exerts over fiction the repressive power she has tried to exert over Art. Things as they are – human nature as it is – the conflict always going on between law and passion, the individual and society – she will not have spoken of.'[14] Linton bemoaned the dearth of realistic fiction in England because of the way in which it is standardized for one reader (the Young Person), and called for a 'specialised literature' of 'truth to human nature'.

Women continued to challenge the polite association between private and public by mobilizing the idea of 'decent science' in order to assert the right of girls and women to be educated into knowledge of female sexual health, whether through fictional narratives such as the contrasting fates of Evadne and Edith in

Grand's *The Heavenly Twins,* the factual language of plant biology in the children's primers on sex-education of Ellis Ethelmer,[15] or the physiology pamphlets for adults produced by health reformers such as Ada S. Ballin, editor of the journal *Womanhood.*[16] In 1894 the *New Review* featured a symposium entitled 'The Tree of Knowledge'.[17] This discussion on sex education and the treatment of sexual relationships in fiction registers a range of contemporary perspectives from participants with a literary, cultural or religious profile in public life, including Thomas Hardy, E. L. Linton and Sarah Grand.[18] In June 1894 the feminist paper the *Signal,* responding to the symposium in its regular feature 'Between the Lights', a witty, epigrammatic, dialogue between a Wildean cast of female characters on the 'woman question' of the month – 'the tree of knowledge'– summarized the debate. The 'Woman of No Importance' (her moniker drawn from the eponymous mother from Oscar Wilde's 1893 play), contends that the unmarried girl should not be blindfolded. ' "Blindfolded! God forbid! I would give her spectacles", exclaimed the Advanced Woman. "Yes, and science primers as well" the Society Dame mocked. "And why not?" asked the Woman of No Importance ". . . decent science is infinitely preferable to indecent suggestion".'[19] Scientific and medical knowledge of sexual reproduction and disease was championed by many New Woman novelists, most notably Sarah Grand, who had contributed to the forum on 'The Tree of Knowledge'. The assertion of 'the mother' reflects the argument of many feminists for whom scientific discourse, although traditionally a masculine province, could make sex education acceptable both in the home to enlighten both mother and daughter, and in the public sphere to enable and inform debate.

Girls' ignorance of sexual matters was defended by many anti-New Woman writers like Lady Jeune, in an article in the *Fortnightly Review,* 'The Revolt of the Daughters',[20] a reply to Mrs Crackenthorpe's article in the *Nineteenth Century.*[21] In the interest of maintaining the Victorian 'angel' figure she clung to an ideal of girlhood as intrinsically ignorant (and thus powerless), hoping that we should 'lose something of the robust intellectual self-reliance of emancipated girls', that we might always have 'the daughters of our hearts, ignorant, wilful, perhaps not always prudent [but with] a belief in the illusions of life'. In expressing her fear of giving girls 'knowledge of life' she exercises the lexicon of conservative male literary critics, asking if society wishes, 'to see our girls half men in theory and half women in inexperience and ignorance [?]'[22]

New Woman writers who approached questions of sexual relations in their fiction were struggling in the confines of a central paradox: to keep their claim to 'womanly' femininity at the same time as their critics discredited and denounced them as 'unsexing' themselves. New Woman writers' aim was to inform and persuade their readers of their own moral and ideological agenda with their novels with a purpose, and to invest themselves with the status of moral guardians. Writing of the new novels by women in 'The Strike of a Sex', William Barry in the *Quarterly Review* insisted that whilst

> It may suit M. Zola to confound the tragic and the pathological; in art there is a degree of mental as of physical agony which must not be shown, or the audience will turn away their eyes. Let the asylum, the sickbed, keep its dreadful secrets; the curtain which divides them from the art of literature, is happily, impenetrable.[23]

In the same year, 1894, an article in the feminist *Woman's Signal*, declared the 'modern woman' heroine of the new novels 'unmaternal, fierce towards her sex-conditions, wildly bent on selfish development or selfish pleasures'; the writer begs '[i]f all this is real life, hide it away in clinics',[24] a comment which is uncomfortably close to reflecting the situation of the incarceration of women in asylums who were held to be 'mad', socially or sexually deviant.[25] Yet Barry, and other conservative critics, were fighting against the tide.

In direct contrast to their critics' accusations of degeneration, social purity New Woman writers' mission was supremely moral: to make healthy and hygienic the male-authored narrative, to take on taboo subjects, and inform young women of the dangers of married life. Their discourses of health, fitness and purity combining moral counsel with stylistic or formal concerns can be seen in relation to the cultural standing its producers sought to gain. Writing which was seen as a subtly-acting medicine or tonic – rather than strident polemic or moralizing edification – published in the appropriate cultural canons, attained a greater social acceptance and literary merit.

In their role as educators, and in shaping a feminist aesthetic in direct resistance to the Aesthetes, writers such as Grand also wrote to consolidate a national culture. In her 'Candour in English Fiction', E. L. Linton took up George Moore's metaphor of literature as a nutriment acting as the cultural fortifier and consolidator of national hegemony. Commenting on the censorship of the novel made fit for the young reader, she asks '[m]ust men go without meat because babes must be fed with milk? Or, because men must have meat, shall the babes be poisoned with food too strong for them to digest?'[26] Her analogy of cultural consumption is developed through a dialectic with imperialism: she remarks upon the 'queer anomaly of a strong-headed and masculine nation cherishing a feeble, futile, milk-and-water literature – of a truthful and straightforward race accepting the most transparent humbug as a picture of human life'.[27] This image of the infantilization of the State, and demise of culture linking the strength of the race with its national culture, can be seen in the international context of competition for imperialist powers. Linton's rhetoric of a literary nationalism demands that to produce a virile, 'strong-headed' literature we must break away from the narrow confines of Grundyism, and its degenerating influence upon British culture. Her solution was the 'locked bookcase' to protect the young person, so that 'mature men and women should not sacrifice truth and common-sense in literature'[28] for the sake of the young reader.

The urgent task of imparting realism to contemporary literature in Britain was informed by opposition to the movement in French Naturalist fiction, a disavowal of an influence of a movement whose interest in the biological motivations of human behaviour and theories of heredity had opened up questions of the representation of sex and marital relations in fiction.[29] This consolidation of a popular cultural form was imagined as building the resistance and defences of the national body against contamination by foreign invasion/penetration, and subsequent degeneration.

The dichotomy between 'high' and 'low' forms, 'art' and 'purpose', was gendered, as we have seen in Gosse's division of poetry and the novel, so some women writers sought to differentiate the moral aims of their literary projects from those of male decadents and aesthetes in a national context. In Sarah

Grand's *The Beth Book*, Galbraith, the authoritative male doctor who had featured in *The Heavenly Twins*, and mentor to Beth, remarks: 'If France is to be judged by the tendency of its literature and art at present, one would suppose it to be dominated and doomed to destruction by a gang of lascivious authors and artists who are sapping the manhood of the country and degrading the womanhood by idealising self-indulgence and mean intrigue' (*BB* 367). The moral values of Beth's writing project are frequently distinguished from those of French literature which is associated with naturalism, decadence, symbolism and aestheticism. The cultural invasion of these forms in the English literary marketplace constitutes a threat of contamination to the purity of the English novel promised by feminist writers.

Critics have accounted for the expulsion of the French novel from such English texts as part of the imperial project of consolidating the national culture. Teresa Mangum suggests that in her references to French novels in *The Beth Book*, Grand 'plays on the English sense of *national* superiority to foreigners by aligning her work with "Britishness"'.[30] Angelique Richardson argues more strongly that Grand's aims express an explicit imperialist racism: 'French literature was a metonymic figuring of racial impurity; the English novel had to be purged of such damaging racial influences before it could serve the British empire.'[31]

Late nineteenth-century debates on literary value and national culture take on a dialogic form between Beth and her former childhood friend, Alfred Cayley Pounce, who as an adult has been corrupted by a patriarchal, Decadent art-world and the immorality it fosters. In Pounce's characterization as an aspiring stylist and reviewer for fictive journal the *Patriarch*, an attack is mounted on the art of the Decadents – synonymous here with the dominant, or high culture – on the grounds of their sensuality and the apoliticism of their preoccupation with style. Pounce's corrupt morals are expressed in his wish that Beth be George Sand to his Alfred de Musset, a relationship which combines a personal morality with a French aesthetic of which Grand does not approve. Beth persistently rejects the preoccupations of style in fiction as socially and morally irresponsible: '[m]anner has always been less to me than matter. When I think of all the preventable sin and misery there is in the world, I pray

28

God give us books of good intention – never mind the style!' (*BB* 460), an expostulation which leaves the reader in no doubt of the author's didactic principles. Although the New Woman writers had benefited from the way in which French writers had opened up new ways for writing about sexual relations and representing sexuality in fiction, for the moral purity feminist that Grand was, this debt was to be fervently disavowed if she was to distance her ethical project from the degeneracy and sexual permissiveness associated with the French in the mind of the reading public.

If the feisty, forthright and articulate protagonist Beth in the semi-autobiographical *The Beth Book* is instrumental as a mouthpiece for the cultural and moral values of Grand's particular literary project, she also belongs to a significant strand in this body of fiction which depicts the working life of the independent, autonomous woman writer. Grand's *bildungsroman*, as well as exploring Beth's formative childhood experiences, charts the growth of the adult aspirations which result in a writing and public-speaking career, and develops a detailed picture of her thoughts and work in her 'secret chamber', and later the frugal lifestyle of her 'attic home'.

The figure of the female artist features in a number of New Woman texts and often stands for a professional woman and her marginalized position in society. In Mary Cholmondeley's *Red Pottage* (1899) Hester Gresley is a writer, as is Janet Suttaby in Mabel Emily Wotton's 'The Fifth Edition' (1896), Bridget Ruan in Netta Syrett's *Nobody's Fault* (1896), Mary Erle in Ella Hepworth Dixon's *The Story of a Modern Woman* (1894) and Cosima Chudleigh in George Paston's (Emily Morse Symonds) *A Writer of Books* (1899); and in Paston's *A Modern Amazon* (1894) Regina Haughton is a journalist. In Mona Caird's *The Daughters of Danaus* Hadria Fullerton is a musician and Valeria Du Prel a published writer. As Chapter 1 has suggested, the city was a vital facet of the modernity of the New Woman and her entry into the public realm. In this section we consider the depiction of female writers' struggle for a professional identity in relation to contemporary debates on literary value, the artist and the genius. Readings of the latter two novels will consider how the relationship between the metropolis and the female artist figure addressed feminist concerns: the aesthetic and cultural values to which she subscribes, and the circumstances and constraints against her in her quest for selfhood – those of the conflicting pressures of domesticity and Grub Street.

In the 1890s more women were becoming more visible in the public domain in employment and leisure. There were more spaces opening to women consumers including the new department stores; literary and other Clubs; women-only restaurants; cafés and tearooms, some of which catered to the vegetarian New Woman. Assisted by access to public transport,[32] middle-class women enjoyed leisure time in a new way, and benefited from places for public intercourse with other women to develop both personal and professional networks. The woman who walked, and wrote about the public streets, was removed from the domestic, private space traditional to the Victorian middle-class woman, and challenged cultural norms about markers of social and class identity. 'Platform Women', such as Florence Fenwick Miller, suffragist campaigners who gave their political speeches in halls and on street corners, were highly visible, public figures who disturbed perceptions of behaviour for middle-class women. They were vilified as unfeminine by the press; an attitude typified in the denigration of such campaigners by a male writer, as 'the unsexed crew that shriek on platforms' (*BB* 509) in *The Beth Book*.

Understanding the *fin-de-siècle* figure of the *flâneur* – the observer and stroller of the modern city – and its availability as a trope to women writers is crucial for how these novels develop their feminist perspectives. Deborah Parsons suggests that the activity of urban observation undertaken by the *flâneur* at the turn of the century is not restricted to the male, and she argues for a 'female city consciousness alternative to that of the male',[33] an urban vision which can be seen in these novels. Her analysis establishes that 'the *flâneur* is not only a historical figure but also a critical metaphor for the characteristic perspective of the modern artist' and therefore that *flânerie* can 'be interpreted as an attempt to identify and place the self in the uncertain environment of modernity'.[34] Therefore it is through this appropriation of the position of the *flâneur* – as *flâneuse* – that the women writer and artist protagonists of these novels are enabled to give us a subjective, feminist perspective within the social relations of the city.

30

In situating their heroines in the cityscape, New Woman writers highlighted their relationship to other urban social types of women such as prostitutes, shop girls and typists, the charity worker and philanthropist, as recent scholarship has suggested.[35] When such New Women live connected lives with the working classes in this way, identifications are made, and a form of feminist solidarity and social responsibility explored. The shop girl, Monica Madden in George Gissing's *The Odd Women* (1893) who meets her prospective husband, Edmund Widdowson, while out unchaperoned by the river in Richmond, risks compromising her respectability in making such an unconventional liaison. It is only circumstance and economic necessity which determine the parallels with and differences between the emancipated New Woman figures and the prostitute in this, and other texts. Miss Eade, Monica's former colleague at the draper's shop, becomes a prostitute at Victoria Station, 'a not unimportant type of the odd woman' (*The Odd Women* 299), whilst Monica is married to the possessive and controlling Widdowson.

In *The Story of A Modern Woman* Mary Erle's friend, Alison, daughter of society figure, Lady Jane Ives, is a philanthropist who lives by her principles; her belief in solidarity of sisterhood is enacted in her befriending and support of poor new mothers in a flat in Mayfair. In one episode, Mary accompanies Alison in her support work to the hospital in order to observe 'life' for her writing; from this aesthetic desire to produce social realism, Mary's observations lead her to a political empathy and female solidarity. Mary discovers the story behind a patient, 'Number Twenty Seven', a shop girl; Dr Dunlop Strange, Alison Ives' lover, has seduced the girl, who then tried to commit suicide in the canal, but subsequently dies in hospital. When Alison contracts a disease from her and also dies, the girl's story underlines the shared sexual oppression of women and the risks of seduction and abandonment of women in the city.

In *A Writer of Books* the eponymous protagonist Cosima Chudleigh observes the life of the city with something of the enquiring gaze of the Naturalist writer, like a physician whose dissection is the analysis of their subjects. This model of the writer/reporter may enact social detachment, but in Paston's text the effect is rather to create social conscience and awareness of female oppression. The freedom of the *flâneur* on the street can accord, and be an effect of, a privileged perspective and power, so we see the artistic 'gaze' control what it observes and records. Whilst walking alone down Regent Street after leaving a concert, Cosima is followed and approached by a young man, yet the relationship of power is reversed, and rather than be the passive object of his flirtatious 'glance', as a writer, she positions herself as the observer, and looks back. She accepts his invitation to go for dinner with him, but the ensuing conversation is motivated by Cosima's 'scientific' enquiries into the customs of a different social class: 'keener than her hunger was her desire to continue her study of this type of youth, and as a scientific spectator, to see something of a phase of life which is mostly shuttered off with jealous care from the knowledge of the girl from whom the wife is bred, as distinct as from the girl from whom the social scapegoat is bred' (*Writer of Books* 41). Through their encounter, she meets with the waitress Bess and her dramatic story of female exploitation and revenge. It is Cosima's unchaperoned status, as writer/observer that enables her to gain access to experience her subjectivity differently, and to reveal to the reader the aesthetic framework of the 'scientific spectator' for whom gaining objective knowledge is both an intellectual and political ideal.

The defence of (male) artistic integrity was a common discourse in late-Victorian fiction; it pitted journalism against the artist and the novel, the commodity of the mass literary market against the true expression of individuality. It is typified in Gissing's *New Grub Street* (1891), where the organic instinct of the writer battling against commercialism has its apotheosis in the impoverished but brilliant Edwin Reardon. Gissing also describes exploitative relationships for women in the literary market; Dora and Maud Milvain write and review for women's papers to support themselves, and Marian Yule is powerless under her father's tyrannical work schedule, and an unacknowledged researcher in his publications. Toiling in the Reading Room of the British Museum one day, Marian feels herself to be an automaton, as she identifies herself with a mechanical commodity she sees advertised: a 'Literary Machine' (*New Grub Street* 138), producing work in conditions from which her economic and creative autonomy have been stripped.

In *The Story of a Modern Woman*, once orphaned, Mary moves to London and becomes a journalist and illustrator/painter, but is obliged to compromise her ambitions by writing popular romance to make her money. The conditions for literary and creative production are described as inhospitable to the woman artist. The editor of *Illustrations* dismissively suggests to her that ' "[w]ith practice, you may be able to write stories which other young ladies like to read" ' (*SMW* 107). Mary must rewrite her story of a clandestine affair along lines suited to the supposedly censorial British reading public: ' "It – won't do?" faltered Mary. "Why I've written just as you told me. There's a ball in the first volume, a parting in the second" ' (*SMW* 184); she discovers that it is the *'banal*, the pretty-pretty, the obvious! This was what she was to write – if she wanted to make any money, to keep her head above water' (*SMW* 183). Sally Ledger has suggested that the editor's remarks do not reflect the commercial possibilities for women in the burgeoning mass media which women were entering, the new journalism, and a literary marketplace in which realist novels by women enjoyed some economic success. Ledger argues that Hepworth Dixon's 'pessimistic aesthetic vision of women being economically driven to churn out anodyne romantic fiction . . . is somewhat overstated given the fact that her own novel . . . like the novels of Sarah Grand and Mona Caird, is by no means a "pretty story", yet was a commercial success'.[36] The vision in this novel is a pessimistic one, it participates in the contemporary protest about the market conditions for creativity, but in emphasizing failure, perhaps seeks to register the magnitude of the achievement of women in their struggle for professional status and intellectual autonomy.

We see the London life of over-work, single living, poor diet and stress invariably takes its toll on heroines. In *The Beth Book*, selflessly caring for Arthur Brock a fellow artist, Beth's privations mean fatigue and starvation. As a newcomer to London, looking out over the city in *The Story of a Modern Woman*, Mary Erle had reassured her younger brother and herself, ' "[w]e're not going to be afraid of it – just because it's big, and brutal, and strong" ' (*SMW* 10). Later, her doctor pronounces Mary anaemic and a 'bundle of nerves' and protests: ' "All you young ladies ought to be living a healthy, out-of-door life, happily married, and with no mental worries!" ' (*SMW* 183). As in *New Grub Street*, the Darwinian 'struggle for survival' increasingly informs

Mary's experience as a struggling writer and independent woman: 'her brain was busy with two over powering thoughts, the awful struggle with death, the protest against annihilation . . . and the fact that henceforward she was to walk alone, to fight the battle of life unaided – a moral starveling, whose natural instincts were to be pinched, repressed and neatly trimmed in conformity with the rules of the higher civilisation' (*SMW* 228). Her hopes of becoming an artist are finally destroyed by the forces of the city

> that lay stretched out at her feet; majestic, awe-inspiring, inexorable, triumphant London . . . Standing alone, there on the heights, she made a feint as if to grasp the city spread out before her, but the movement ended in a vain gesture, and the radiance of her face was blotted out as she began to plod homewards in the twilight of the suburban road. (*SMW* 273)

The London flat where she thought, dreamed, and wrote, represented an escape from domesticity, a possibility of independence beyond parental and marital homes symbolized in the 'latchkey' motif which featured on the covers of Lane's Keynote series and elsewhere in imagery associated with the New Woman. Such a space resonated with the feminine; Ann Heilmann reads this creative female space as a 'metaphorical conflation of room with womb', which she considers to be a 'central paradigm in New Woman fiction',[37] away from the confines and view of patriarchal interferences. But the private garret room of the artist-philosopher is also mapped onto the division between the individual and the city street of the masses. The hidden attic as a retreat from the worldly, traditionally the haunt of the romantic and impoverished genius, also appealed to women writers. When in *The Beth Book* Beth takes an attic room in Bayswater, it is her own version of a private and quiet domesticity conducive to work: 'once settled in her attic home, she returned to the healthy, regular, industrious habits which had helped her so much in the days when she had been at her best' (*BB* 490), but also gives her a 'hallowed seclusion' (*BB* 524) consistent with her depiction as a visionary artist figure. By largely confining woman writer, Beth, to her garret room during her period in London – unlike Paston or Hepworth Dixon, Grand does not depict her heroine exploring the bustle of the city –

Grand draws on the romantic conception of the artist, outside of the vulgar metropolitan crowd.

The debates over 'genius', and the struggles over 'pure art' and the commercial, which consolidate values of the literary market place had particular significance for the female author seeking to claim a high status position without compromising the polemical and political medium and message of feminism. For women writers the idea of the 'female genius' could be used to mobilize protest for greater opportunities for middle-class women's access to education, work, and the social sphere, as did, for example, Hepworth Dixon (1894), Paston (1898), and Cholmondeley (1899).

'Genius', in its reconfigurement by evolutionary science was a significant register of ideas of both 'racial' progress and degeneracy – what it consisted of, how one came to possess it, and who could claim it, was fiercely contested between feminists, eugenicists, and the other cultural critics of degeneration. The notion of the 'woman of genius' was therefore a contested one of considerable importance to establishing the legitimacy of female participation in national cultural production. Leading theories of genius – particularly those which were re-evaluating the term in the light of eugenics after Francis Galton's *Hereditary Genius: An Inquiry into its Laws and Consequences* (1869) – held that it was a hereditary quality which would therefore express itself in whatever field it was peculiar to, regardless of the will of the individual.[38]

There was a need for feminists to lay claim to the subjectivity of genius as a negotiation out of the restrictive limits in which scientific explanations of creativity would circumscribe their gender; Grand and Caird were not atypical amongst feminist writers in seeking to appropriate not only cultural legitimacy for women's artistic and intellectual status, but its apotheosis, genius. Penny Boumelha in an excellent discussion on women writers and cultural values argues that in the late Victorian woman writer's novel, 'genius' is held to be 'not earned, developed by hard work, or sought by ambition'[39] but there are modifications and exceptions to this view to be found; for example, both Beth and Hadria must undertake a lengthy apprenticeship of hard work which builds on their innate, hereditary 'genius'.

35

The predominant romantic notions that 'genius' was the exuberant expression of an irrepressible, vital force, but must be disciplined, or risk running to obsessive madness were contradictions to be reconciled in the modern construction of the 'genius'. The aestheticist Vernon Lee for example, writing from a position in direct contrast to Mona Caird, optimistically claimed that 'genius, like murder, *would out*; for genius is one of the liveliest forces of nature: not to be quelled or quenched, adaptable, protean, expansive, nay explosive ... Hence, to my mind there are *no mute inglorious Miltons*, or none worth taking into account'[40] (italics in original). Lee stressed the ways in which genius is at odds with the art of the mechanical modern age and thus indifferent to the commercial demands of market forces. The ability of Hadria Fullerton, the 'woman of genius' in Caird's third novel, *The Daughters of Danaus* (1894), it is suggested, has an organic basis, but the struggle to survive and succeed against the restrictions and obstacles stacked against her by a cultural tyranny proves a stronger force than nature.

In the opening pages Hadria and her siblings debate the claim of American philosopher, Ralph Waldo Emerson (1803–82) which will be the linchpin of the novel: artistic power will out and prove itself, whatever the given circumstances. Hadria argues: 'There is nothing to prove that thousands have not been swamped by maladjustment of character to circumstance, and I would even go so far as to suggest that perhaps the very greatest of all are those whom the world has never known, because the present conditions are inharmonious with the very noblest and the very highest qualities' (*DD* 11). Unlike Vernon Lee's adaptable 'genius', for Caird, genius will not 'out'; those 'mute, inglorious Miltons' are specifically female, the 'woman of genius' can be stifled, her self-expression curbed by long-continued neglect or oppression. Like Virginia Woolf's scenario in which it is the contemporary Jacobean society of 'Judith', imaginary sister of Shakespeare, that disallows her literary production, such barriers make the evidence for female genius, for Hadria, hard to prove for there have been few successes: 'poor things – pale hypotheses nameless peradventures – lie in forgotten churchyards – unthought of, unthanked, untrumpeted, and all their tragedy is lost in the everlasting silence' (*DD* 13).

Ultimately, Hadria is denied the possibility of sustaining a demanding career because she sacrifices herself to her duties as a daughter, mother and wife, and her musical 'genius' as composer and pianist will be unknown to the world. The conflict between personal and professional roles, internalized notions of the social norms of familial duties is common to Netta Syrett's 'Keynotes' novel of 1896, *Nobody's Fault*, which charts the career of a disappointed young woman, Bridget Ruan, who achieves her aim to become a school teacher, only to become stifled by the vocation, and then turn to writing. After her first novel is published her chances of happiness as a writer, and living with her lover, are eventually abandoned after her father's death in order to return home to support her bereaved and sick mother. The title of the story points toward how Bridget's agency is determined by hegemonic forces, so that her decision to be her mother's carer, and consequent personal tragedy as failed artist is said to be 'nobody's fault'. The novel is unusual in its theme of class mobility, a portrayal of a New Woman who is of working-class origins and whose career estranges her from her publican parents, yet is also unable to fit into upper middle-class society.

Ann Heilmann has argued that, as with the representation of the female protagonist as failed artist in other New Woman realist texts which are plotted onto the 'male' genre of the *Künstlerroman*, Caird's explanation of Hadria's failure participates in the belief that the heroine is 'predestined to fail precisely because she has the making of an artist: deep feeling and a capacity for infinite absorption'.[41]

The notion of the artist as an essentially tragic figure, doomed to struggle in a mercenary world because of his/her possession of a heightened, spiritual sensibility is one which clearly offers a cache of cultural value to the female author writing in this genre. Yet for Caird the central conflict for the protagonist of her *Künstlerroman* which leads to tragic failure, is between private and public roles; the demands which Hadria's personal life make determine her professional achievements. The conflict between work and motherhood, creativity and procreativity is a significant one for much of this fiction. Margaret Morganroth Gullette has argued that in choosing a tragedy of 'unhappy survival' rather than doomed suicide for her heroine Hadria, Caird is imagining an alternative fate for transgressive women, breaking with a tradition of deaths for heroines from Gustave Flaubert's *Madame Bovary* (1857) to George Eliot's *The Mill on the Floss* (1860).[42] Gullette reads Hadria's 'high minded failure' positively because it leaves the reader with an open and inconclusive ending.

The figure of the struggling 'genius' author receives endorsement in Grand's characterization of Beth in *The Beth Book*. The repudiation of society's laurels and of material gain, so contradictory to the aims of true art, vindicates the woman writer, especially the autobiographer, from being unwomanly because seeking to gain approbation and recognition: '[s]he had no amateur impatience to appear in print and become known ... she was not one to glory in public successes, however great' (*BB* 453).[43]

Even if Grand's ostensible purpose in writing her novels was polemic, rather than aesthetic, a portrayal of the female artistic genius which gives her cultural legitimacy, necessitates an engagement with the literary values of 'high art'. In her short story, 'The Undefinable: A Fantasia' (1908)[44] the concept of the female genius as a gatekeeper of national culture is explored in an allegory, a retelling of the Pygmalion myth, a central narrative in late nineteenth-century art and literature, such as in Edward Burne-Jones's series (1868–78) accompanying William Morris's *The Earthly Paradise* (1868), and in Vernon Lee's short story, discussed in Chapter 3. An encounter between a male artist and a female model reworks the definitions of 'genius', muse and art, with the reformation of the male artist through the guiding genius/influence of the female muse.[45] Unlike the lengthy *Künstlerroman*, *The Beth Book*, the short story form allows Grand to exploit witty dialogue to develop her outspoken and brash New Woman genius character.

The boundary between art and life is crucial – how does life pollute or affect art and culture and vice versa? A *female* economy of cultural production emerges in which temperance and purity must be practised in contrast to a *male* physical economy of decadent appetites and excessive 'spending'. The woman instructs the male artist in the proper path to artistic productivity; ' "you must wait, you know, to recover yourself. You've lost such a lot" ' ('TU' 269). Sublimation of sexual energy into artistic production has long been associated with the (male) genius; the social purist deploys it in order not to refute the association but to transfigure it into an economy of purity, as opposed to the physical sensation-seeking of the Decadents.

The vision of genius here is restricted to the confines of disciplinary discourses of social purity in the management of the body, those which express concern for a healthy, non-sensuous art – rather than one of the establishment 'fleshly school' or Decadent, one of Grand's chief targets. Whilst this allegory is ostensibly about male art, it is also about empowering the female through a positive re-evaluation of a feminine, spiritual, sensibility. For Grand, it is this spiritual and moral dimension of life which art should represent. Despite the New Woman's rigorous moral proscriptions, genius remains 'undefinable', an elusive quality which bespeaks an artistic autonomy apart from the vulgarity of bourgeois markets and of the limited perspective of the working-class artisan, the frame maker of the story.

In producing new moral values for their literary production and intervention into masculinist forms and values, New Woman writers were divided on class politics, and much work reproduced the values of the dominant social order in that it presupposed its capitalist structures, with the exception of the utopianism of Florence Caroline Dixie, Margaret Harkness, Jane Hume Clapperton, or the American, Charlotte Perkins Gilman. Feminist reformers were determined to offer alternative views of the role of fiction, and were part of the wider cultural debate for new subjects to be addressed in the novel with a greater realism. Whilst they produced distinctive visions and values, they were divided on what the new femininity should be. Portraits of female genius were important to counter the prevailing status reserved for literary men; in this way they marked themselves out as leaders and innovators in the society, a national contribution beyond their progenitive role. They rebutted strong accusations of degeneracy in the various treatments of female sexuality which abounded in their work, and called for the entitlement of women to an autonomy beyond that allowed by current patriarchal laws and values. We will see in the next chapter how these themes were treated and the literary forms these took in the work of a number of New Woman writers.

3

New Woman Writers' Works

As we have outlined in Chapter 1, there were many identities subsumed in the term New Woman at the *fin de siècle*. This chapter will illustrate some of the variety of literary forms and genres that New Women appropriated and transformed, and will explore if and how these enabled them to express their feminist goals and other intellectual aims. As well as mapping some of the thematic and formal differences between texts, this chapter will trace converging ideological strands, and the writers' shared concerns and values around marriage, motherhood, sexuality and identity in relation to imperialism.

The early feminist campaigns lead by Josephine Butler against the Contagious Diseases Acts (1864, 1866, 1869) and the conditions and civil liberties of prostitution were focused on moral reform and the marriage question. Not all women who campaigned for social and political power saw this as incompatible with their 'womanly' and socially sanctioned roles as wives and mothers. On the contrary, these identities would be reconstructed within the language of social and moral purity by campaigners who critiqued the dichotomy of career and marriage. In addition to those pressing for premarital chastity for men as well as women, there was a significant group of intellectuals, such as Annie Besant and Charles Bradlaugh, agitating not only for greater knowledge of sex relations for young women and men (as some of the social purity campaigners did), but also – as did the Malthusian League (founded 1877) – for advocacy of 'preventive checks', or contraceptive practices for use within and out of marriage.[1]

The linkage of femininity with modernity as an organic outcome to the natural process of evolution is central to the New

Woman's sociocultural representation. In the rhetoric of feminists of the *fin de siècle*, modern femininity is the natural, hence inevitable, outcome of the processes of evolutionary change. Yet as we have seen, her opponents argued that the New Woman was unnatural, an aberration symptomatic of degeneration and heralding social decay – precisely the opposite of that progressive, regenerative 'womanly' role which feminists argued for her. Feminist interpretations of the theory of sexual selection which featured so centrally in Darwin's *The Descent of Man and Selection in Relation to Sex* (1871) conferred a new agency upon women in determining the fitness of the coming 'race'; by choosing the best, healthiest partners, women would reform men and marriage. Woman's investment in such ideas was precarious, because, for example, many male commentators argued that her proximity to nature meant that sexual maternity was her only role in contributing to national progress. But, as we will see, configurations of sexual and racial maternity were deeply appealing to very many New Woman writers and thinkers because they so compellingly situated women as unique in their power as citizens in being able to determine the progress of their society.

'Moral' eugenic discourse became a crucial strand emerging from the campaigns of the social purity feminists. This was in part precipitated by a shift in the understanding of disease fostered by evolutionary biology – most crucially through August Weismann's theory of the transmission of the germ-plasm whose lectures on heredity were published in the *Fortnightly Review* during 1883. The continuity of the immutable germ-plasm provided the causal basis for the relation between ancestor and descendant, rather than only between parent and offspring.[2]

Putting paid to older, vitalist notions of life forces, it provided a materialist basis for understanding organic matter, and in particular, understanding of the way in which diseases like syphilis were not only carried by the individual body, but had intergenerational transmission via the heredity of the body through the germ-cell, or primary unit of heredity (today, what we know as the gene). With the individual's ineluctable heredity becoming a new locus for disease, for purity feminists then, contamination could be located within the promiscuous male body and men held at fault for the sickness of the social body. Men were taken to task for their responsibility in the spread of disease at the same time as for a hypocritical morality.

In the 1880s, new scientific research proved that syphilis was a bacterium that, once contracted, could remain latent in the body without presenting symptoms. Unknowing women could marry apparently 'reformed rakes', and become infected. Contagious parents could pass on the disease to the unborn child; once it manifested itself congenitally it was at the secondary stage. The effects of syphilis at the tertiary stage affected the brain, and frequently produced symptoms of insanity. Estimates show that 70 per cent of the male asylum population were syphilitic, and suffering from general paralysis, the terminal stage of the disease. Elaine Showalter has argued that syphilis was actually in decline in the 1890s,[3] yet it formed a significant anxiety for society. A Royal Commission report of 1916 suggested that 10 per cent of men were estimated to have syphilis, and a higher number to have gonorrhoea; it remained incurable until the 1940s.

The authors of New Woman fiction aimed to expose the impurity of male sexuality, the sexual double standards and hypocrisy of marriage through their plots, and to reform the traditional formal confines of the 'unhealthy' male-authored romances.[4] In particular, the 'syphilis plot' of such novels depicted the risky transaction of marriage for innocent young women and the gruesome consequences for their children. Sarah Grand's fiction explores the possibilities of female emancipation in the public sphere of education and career, whilst endorsing marriage as 'the most sacred institution in the world'[5] and as exacting motherhood of the highest standard by the sexually selective 'Women of the Future'. Her belief in female evolutionary superiority was often expressed in a moral eugenics which sought the regeneration of the race and nation, and came perilously close to the contemporary imperialist and patriarchal rhetoric of women's role as the bearers of the race. Social purity feminism was deeply flawed by ideological inconsistencies: it challenged the present sex essentialism by arguing that men, and indeed humanity, could be changed and improved, yet replaced it with its own brand of essentialism in its insistence on innate male (moral and spiritual) inferiority and women's innate superiority.

Grand's triple-decker novel *The Heavenly Twins* (1893) warned of the dangers of sexual infection and its hereditary consequences for the upper middle-class wife and her family. Its frank treatment of venereal disease and extramarital relations was shocking to many reviewers, but it was celebrated by Margaret Shurmer Sibthorp in *Shafts*, as a novel of 'immortal power'.[6] The unapologetic didacticism of the novel – one of the primary criticisms it received in the press[7] – was valued by Sibthorp for taking in hand the education of the public in a new morality. The parallel stories of Edith Beale and her friend, Evadne Frayling, who are both married off to dissolute army officers – Major Colquhoun and Sir Mosely Monteith – illustrate the perils of a sexually ignorant middle-class femininity. Evadne is an autodidact whose reading of French novels and physiology textbooks combined with investigation into Monteith's dissolute past, has taught her to keep her marriage unconsummated. As a mouthpiece for her author's eugenicist beliefs, she opines: ' "[i]t is the system that is at fault, the laxity which permits anyone, however unfit, to enter upon the most sacred of all human relations" ' (*THT*). Her conclusion implies the desire for state regulation of marriage that Francis Galton advocated.[8]

Grand's short stories also addressed the social and moral responsibility of marriage. The short stories of family fortunes in the collection, *Our Manifold Nature* (1894) register the shift in cultural discourse during the nineteenth century from genealogy to a preoccupation with heredity. In 'Boomellen, A Study from Life', which first appeared in the *Temple Bar* in 1892, the narrator relates the short and 'ineffectual life' of a dissolute young man of the landed gentry given to bouts of drinking, lethargy and loitering with peasant girls. Boomellen's family genealogy is chequered with undesirables: 'his Father had been "wild" in his youth, but his degrading habits were cut short by something which suspiciously resembled epilepsy' (*OMN* 353). Sexual immorality and sensual excess are linked with somatic or psychological dysfunction here; the reading public understood this equation of badness with madness. However, as Grand's stories repeatedly rehearse, biological responsibility ultimately lies with the mother, with her female power of sexual selection. Boomellen's mother's exalted piety leads her to believe – mistakenly – that she is saving the soul of a reprobate by marrying his father. Boomellen's last act is to swim out in a stormy sea in a clearly vain attempt to rescue shipwrecked passengers. The ending is a closure on a crisis of power, which has put into question his masculinity and power as a landowner. In 'Eugenia' the aptly-named eponymous protagonist has inherited her property through her mother's side due to a family curse on sons. When choosing a husband, she rejects the upper-class, degenerate Brinkworthy, and instead selects Saxon Wake, of an old but ascendant family whose struggles to rise above their humble, yeoman origins have improved their offspring's fitness. Saxon's social accomplishments and university education testify to a racial vigour which the canny Eugenia recognizes and rewards. Social regeneration, Grand makes clear, will be achieved though women's agency, their economic independence, and their eugenic decisions.

The goal of female sexual selection was also a concern of other New Woman writers, such as Emma Frances Brooke, who shared the desire that sexually selective women become national regenerators through their motherhood, but proposed quite different means to achieve it. Brooke's interest in an assertive femininity and sexuality autonomous from marriage, was explored in her novels. A reviewer in *Shafts* found Emma Brooke's triple-decker, *Life the Accuser* (1896) to be too preoccupied with its Amazonian New Woman heroine Rosalie's sexuality: '[i]t lays too much emphasis upon, and exalts into too much importance the physical, forgetting that though the physical part of our complex nature must have consideration, yet must it be held in its own place, and its place is to be dominated by the mental and spiritual.'[9] For whilst Brooke, like Grand, was concerned with a eugenic agenda, unlike the social purity feminists, the greater autonomy and freedom in women's active sexuality in her novels was consistent with an interest in a 'positive' eugenics which held that fitter offspring would be produced through temporary or unofficial sexual relationships.

In Brooke's *A Superfluous Woman* (1894)[10] the high-society heroine Jessamine Halliday flees the excesses of London for the Scottish Highlands, where she meets peasant Colin Macgillvray, and contemplates a 'free-love union', seeking to experience a 'pagan' maternal sexuality. Lady Henry Somerset reviewing in the *Woman's Signal* admits that the novel 'stirs our admiration by a certain undoubted power', but reserves strong criticism for what she sees as simply a role reversal of the romance plot: 'the history of the man attracted by the purity and grace of the country maiden, when, weary of the exotics of civilisation, he turns to the simple charms of the flowers of the fields, is an outworn theme.'[11] Brooke's depiction of the heroine as an exhausted society woman, seeking a fresh and virginal son of the soil is indeed such a revision.[12] Somerset's demand is a significant one: that women writers create new heroines for feminism, in new roles. Yet Brooke's novel depicts a far more troubled and messy experience for her sexually assertive female protagonist than Somerset's review would suggest.

Ann Heilmann reads the Highlands setting in which the sexual feelings and fantasies are experienced in *A Superfluous Woman* as the antithesis of domesticity, 'a natural environment safely removed from the world of social conventions';[13] this is one of the ways in which this setting functions for the heroine's personal development. The rural location is also imagined as a regenerative Nature to escape to, which would restore Jessamine's vitality after the enervating cultural environs of metropolitan aristocratic circles. But her romantic choice of a struggling young farmer with honourable and traditional notions of domesticity leading a life of purity, is for his eugenic fitness: '[h]e was wholesome, from his sunburnt skin to the inmost core of his heart' (*SW* 158). A socialist ethos informs the depiction of the healthy rustic whose class identity is essentialized as a regenerative 'racial' quality.

The lovers have an intimate encounter in the barn: 'the two remained locked in an emotion *apparently* as simple, primitive, and undivided, as though Time had run back for them and borne them to the age of paradise' (*SW* 209, my italics). Brooke historicizes their relationship; Colin, bound by convention, is determined to wait until they are wed to consummate their relationship. Jessamine baulks at the concrete marriage proposal which Colin insists upon – 'All the best gifts he had to offer seemed to her as fetters and a dungeon ... the contract, the contract!' (*SW* 209, 214) and her emancipatory endeavours and fantasy of free love evaporate. Her return to the decayed society life which she had tried to leave behind is complete when she makes a marriage to a syphilitic old aristocrat, the 'effete and dissipated' (*SW* 259) Lord Heriot, 'with his "Hee-hee-hee!" his moist palm, his vile eyes, and his heavily scented apparel' (*SW* 116). She makes the marriage under familial pressure, compounded by hereditary weakness of will, inherited from her Aunt Arabella.[14]

Deploying the gothic tropes of earlier Victorian fiction of the mad relative hidden in the attic, 'the secrets of the House of Heriot' (*SW* 257) soon encompass Jessamine's two syphilitic children who have their nursery in the loft. The dangers of the degenerate heredity of her husband's 'drunken younger brother, of his sister, a microcephalous idiot, of his father dying of paralysis and ungovernable temper' (*SW* 116), become apparent when in a violent outburst Jessamine's 'idiot girl' (*SW* 258) kills her brother.

Like so many other New Woman novels, it ends with the martyr death of the protagonist. The novel's focus on the issue of racial maternity in determining individual and national health and prosperity is tragically and negatively concluded, when on discovering herself to be pregnant again, Jessamine is finally driven to act as a responsible race mother. She induces her own miscarriage and kills herself in the process: '"I will tear my wish out of the centre of things," she cried ... "There is nothing", she said "stronger than a mother"' (*SW* 261). A familiar figure in Victorian fiction, Brooke's infanticidal mother however inaugurates a new icon of tragic heroic maternity (which we will see a version of again in Victoria Cross's *Anna Lombard*) whose final act is dedicated to stemming the tide of degeneracy. The 'civilized' position, outside the law, which Colin had rejected, of the free-loving, unwed parents and the healthy, but illegitimate child, stands for Brooke, as a viable, moral alternative.

The theme of the importance of self-determined motherhood, above and beyond romantic attraction, emerges strongly in Menie Muriel Dowie's novel *Gallia* (1895). Dowie attacks the traditional love-story plot through the development of the ideals and actions of the eponymous heroine, who matches her large 'capacity for mother love' (*Gallia* 129) to her belief in the 'modern health movement' (*Gallia* 115) (for which read, eugenics). Yet Gallia Hamesthwaite does not make the debates of moral and social purity central to her reasoning (for example, she is unperturbed by her prospective husband's past affair with an artists' model, an approach which markedly challenges the demands of purity feminism); she insists that her ideas are separate from the 'boom of women' (*Gallia* 116). The novel explores emotional and psychological registers and their correspondence, or lack of it, to rational selection based on eugenic principles.

Gallia's decisions fall outside the three analytic categories of sexual attraction which her friend Dark Essex identifies from his research into Darwin's work.[15] Her prime concern is to secure a husband who will be most biologically fit for fatherhood, regardless of her feelings for him. Gallia's acceptance of Mark Gurdon's proposal is far from conventional; she frankly states: ' "I must tell you. I am not marrying you because I love you ... But I want to marry; and I want you to be my husband – or rather, the father of my child." ' (*Gallia* 191) She learns later that she was rejected by the man for whom she is honest enough to profess her love, the dysgenic Dark Essex (with his small sallow hands and an hereditary heart condition), out of his respect for her eugenic principles.

The vernacular style of the narrative balances Gallia's serious quest for integrity, emotional and intellectual articulacy, with playful humour and wit. Dowie's representation of assertive female subjectivity, predicated upon eugenic principles, is a radical and transgressive one, depicting as it does a woman's struggles to communicate openly without the prudery or hypocrisy of the previous generation about her choices. Yet whilst Gallia is shown to be a heroine empowered by her independent new principles, the narrative ultimately treads dangerously close to old masculinist values. As a young woman who fell in love with an arrogant chauvinist man who mocked her feminist principles; forgave her husband's dubious sexual past; and succumbed to his desire for her, regardless of whether she felt desire herself, Gallia may well have appealed to unreformed male and female readers, who, like Essex, desired the 'New Woman, who is yet the old!' (*Gallia* 59).

Not all New Woman writers addressed the problems of the Marriage Question with such zeal for eugenic ends, however. For Mona Caird, the New Woman – and Aesthetic – writer and campaigner, writing against the eugenicist agenda of social purity feminists and free love apostles, the radical politics set her apart from many of her contemporaries. She wrote widely on a number of social issues, including animal rights and vivisection. Caird's radical cultural relativism was powerfully voiced in her article on 'Marriage' of 1888[16] and her views were developed in her women's history, *The Morality of Marriage and Other Essays on the Status and Destiny of Woman* (1897). Caird's critique of the institution of marriage and plea for reform built on that of a century earlier; Mary Wollstonecraft had analysed marriage's parallel with prostitution in *Vindication of the Rights of Woman* (1792), and William Thompson and Anna Wheeler's socialist critique *Appeal of One Half of the Human Race, Women Against the Pretensions of the Other Half, Men* was published in 1825. In her book the construct of Nature is Caird's primary subject for attack, yet she aims to bring women under the rubric of evolution: '[women] are treated as if they alone were exempt from the influences of natural selection, of the well-known effects upon organs and aptitudes of continued use or disuse – effects which every one has exemplified in his own life, which every procession proves, and which is freely acknowledged in the discussion of all questions except those in which woman forms an important element' (*MM* 63). Lamarckianism – a theory of the acquisition of new characteristics through environmental influence and the hereditary transmission of use and disuse of certain characteristics – was of especial value to feminist social reformers whose emphasis was upon changing social conditions of circumstance and environment. The older, Lamarckian scientific discourse was contiguous with that of Weismann's new germ-plasm theory of heredity well into the twentieth century, prominent for example in the work of birth control campaigner, Marie Stopes.

Caird's essays treat 'nature' and natural behaviour as a cultural construction; in particular, she protests against the use of terms like 'human nature' and 'woman's nature' which she identifies as historically radically variable because they have a plastic, 'limitless adaptability' (*MM* 186). In a disturbing conceit, a chained but docile dog whose 'nature has adapted itself to the misfortune of captivity' represents the way in which women as a sex have accepted their domestic and social servitude. Her anthropological survey of different cultures and historical periods enables her to argue optimistically for a more fluid account of human behaviour: '[w]e discover that "human nature" need not be a perpetual obstacle to change, to hope, and to progress, as we have hitherto persistently made it; but that it is the very instrument or material through which that change, that hope, and that progress may be achieved' (*MM* 40).

Caird suggests that women's bodies and minds have been damaged by sacrificing their lives to motherhood, and whilst she nominally accepts the (Lamarckian) transmission of nervous complaints and weakened constitutions as hereditary through the female line, she claims that these have become inbred during a long history of female abuse, but are not essentially constitutional to women. Her construction of human identity lays stress on development: gradual evolution in response to environmental pressures.

An opponent of the eugenics advocated by many of her contemporaries, Caird's analysis of marriage and motherhood placed emphasis on the importance of the freedom and rights of the individual, rather than racial health. On the basis of this crucial difference Caird's writing should not be grouped with eugenic New Woman writers like Sarah Grand or Frances Swiney.[17] Lynn Pykett has suggested that Caird is 'perhaps, the classic case of the New Woman writer as both campaigning journalist and fictional polemicist' at the same time as producing novels which are 'self-conscious aesthetic artefacts',[18] signalled through their rhetorical structure and style, their mythological and biblical references, and allusions to classical literature. Pykett identifies Caird's use of ahistoricism in her *Pathway of the Gods* (1898) as a precursor to modernist concerns, such as those developed by D. H. Lawrence.[19] This *fin-de-siècle* mysticism features in Caird's fifth novel, *The Daughters of Danaus* (1894), and links her work with contemporaries in the 'twilight movement' of W. B. Yeats.

The novel's title refers to the Greek myth of the fifty daughters of Danaus: forced into marriage, they murder their husbands on their wedding night and are sentenced to eternally drawing water in sieves from bottomless wells. The myth echoes in the trajectory of the narrative: the destiny of its heroine, Hadria Fullerton, who leaves her husband and escapes the boredom of domestic family life, is only to return to the wives' endless round of daily household duties – 'toiling submissively at their eternal treadmill' (*DD* 207) – at the novel's close. A radical feminist figure, the intellectual and musically talented Hadria ruthlessly criticizes and rejects the staple identities of Victorian womanhood; both the bourgeois ideal of romantic marriage and notion of the fulfilment of motherhood are overturned. Hadria argues that motherhood in the present society is ' "the sign and seal as well as the means and method of a woman's bondage ... a woman with a child in her arms, is, to me, the symbol of an abasement, an indignity, more complete, more disfiguring and terrible, than any form of humiliation that the world has ever seen." ' (*DD* 341) Despite her polemical denunciation of subordination to domesticity, Hadria marries and bears two children early on in the narrative. It is a choice with which Caird breaks from the tradition of the romance plot to explore the development of a modern heroine. A pessimistic confrontation with the present status quo, like many New Woman novels, *The Daughters of Danaus* does not offer solutions to the tragedy of Hadria's thwarted career and unhappy family life, or imagine what a new motherhood might be.

The aesthetics of the late-nineteenth-century literary twilight movement and Celtic renaisscence, for example, in the verse of Fiona Macleod (pseudohym of William Sharp, a close friend of Caird) reworked Matthew Arnold's ideas on the Celtic.[20] The Celtic renascence posited that a Celtic sensibility and nature embodied the values of a spirituality lost to modern, materialistic, English culture. Caird's allegiance to such aesthetic literary values and techniques is demonstrated in her representation of the regenerative power of the Scottish woman of genius. As Chapter 2 outlined, the notion of genius was becoming subjected to analysis of 'race' and national identity,[21] and these debates were incorporated into Caird's presentation of an emotional musicality which leaves Hadria weak to the influence of her peers.

Early on in the story, at a dance held in her local village community Hadria finally agrees – despite her previous refusal – to marry her suitor, Hubert Temperley. The suspension of will that Hadria experiences as an effect of the dance, and the subsequent acceptance of the marriage proposal, derives its narrative effect from the question with which the story is framed, whether there can be free will on the part of the individual, despite heredity and social circumstance. In part, Caird signals, Hadria's capitulation is because of societal pressures and conditions – such as her social proximity to the Temperley family – but her vulnerability is secured through an atavistic state. Hadria's ancestral memory is roused by the wild reels of the Celtic music and their correlative in Nature, the wind in the pines: 'the strangeness of the scene appealed to some wild instinct, and to the intense melancholy that lurks in the Celtic nature' (DD 115).[22] Hadria is dancing Celtic reels before being cornered and harassed by Hubert: '[s]ome mad spirit seemed to possess her. It would appear almost as if she had passed into a different phase of character. She lost caution and care and the sense of external events' (DD 136). This moment acts strategically in the plot to bring about the marriage which Hadria vociferously opposes; the development of the individual is at this juncture overdetermined by heredity. The device of this early, mistaken marriage is necessary to the novel's consideration of the effect of family and marriage upon its heroine. This example does not argue for the fatalism of heredity as a more significant factor than cultural ones in the presentation of individual destiny in The Daughters of Danaus, but highlights Caird's representation of the will in relation to the racial construct of the Celt.

Women's involvement in imperialism and its relation to the race and class politics of eugenics has been highlighted in recent New Woman studies.[23] The new female subjectivities imagined by the largely middle- and upper-class New Woman were often defined in relation to racial and class hierarchies which were inflected with a strong sense of identification with, and investment in, imperialist identities. A key example was Olive Schreiner, whose relationship with imperialism was complex, her life and work contradictory. Like many of her contemporaries, Schreiner's early reading of and interest in the theories of Darwin and the scientific naturalism of Herbert Spencer precipitated a spiritual and intellectual crisis and loss of Christian faith at the same time as they provided a materialist and evolutionary biological understanding of natural and social laws. Her work extensively engages with ideas in evolutionary science, from the passages in Part Two of The Story of an African Farm (1883), to the structural argument for eugenics in Woman and Labour (1911).

51

Pro-Boer in the Anglo-Boer war, Schreiner was also briefly a supporter of Cecil Rhodes, Prime Minister of the Cape, and his policies for British possession in South Africa. However, on her swift disenchantment, her anti-Rhodes allegorical polemic, *Trooper Peter Halkett of Mashonaland* (1897), expressed her bitter opposition to his bloody policies.

Her first novel, *The Story of an African Farm*, was published to great critical acclaim. In its modern narrative method and passages of allegory and dream Schreiner aimed to create a new colonial aesthetic. In the oft-quoted Preface she outlined her literary method, to be not the 'stage method' but that of 'life':

> Here nothing can be prophesied. There is a strange coming and going of feet. Men appear, act and re-act upon each other, and pass away. When the crisis comes the man who would fit it does not return. When the curtain falls no one is ready. When the footlights are brightest they are blown out; and what the name of the play is no one knows. If there sits a spectator who knows, he sits so high that the players in the gaslight cannot hear his breathing. (*AF* 29).

Schreiner suggests that the realism which she is trying to create has not been welcomed in a literary market place that wants Romances, the masculine colonial adventure story. Her book would have been preferred, she claims, 'if it had been a history of wild adventure; of cattle driven into inaccessible "kranzes" by Bushmen; "of encounters with ravening lions, and hair-breadth escapes." This could not be. Such works are best written in Piccadilly or in the Strand: there the gifts of the creative imagination untrammelled by contact with any fact, may spread their wings' (*AF* 29). For a feminist who had grown up in rural South Africa to produce a text real to her colonial experience, from 'the grey pigments around him (sic)', becomes an aesthetic and ideological imperative and responsibility.

Critics have discussed the ideological inconsistencies, even outright colonialism and racism, and their relationship to creative and intellectual innovation in Schreiner's work. Carol Barash has argued of Schreiner that 'her writing attempts to reveal necessary political change but cannot embody those hopes in fiction' and discusses Schreiner's 'ideological concerns as problems of interaction and communication . . . as attempts to narrate, and in the process of narrating to create, a changed world.'[24]

Maternity and its centrality as a positive resource and strength for women, in common with much of the contemporary woman's movement, was key to Schreiner's personal and political vision. Motherhood is significant structurally and thematically in *The Story of An African Farm*: the young heroine Lyndall rails against the one-dimensionality of women's lives for whom marriage is their sole career, and thus on principle she refuses wedlock to the father of her baby. The ideal of the committed relationship without marriage in the context of economic independence which Schreiner upheld, is not realized. Nor does Schreiner imagine a positive conclusion with motherhood in her plot: shortly after the death of her newborn baby, Lyndall dies from grief and illness brought on by exposure.

Schreiner situated maternity in a national, colonial context in the short story 'The Child's Day' (1887) which came to form the introduction to the posthumously published *From Man to Man, or Perhaps Only* (1927), and told of the childhood experiences of Rebekah, a small white girl, from her perspective. The story opens with 'the agony of childbirth': her mother gives birth to twins, one of whom is stillborn. Rebekah's maternal caring instincts are expressed early in her proprietorial relationship to her sisters and struggles with her 'Hottentot' nurse maid, 'Old Ayah', who wishes to keep her away from the babies. Overlapping aspects of gender, class and 'race' identity, and an uneasy identification with colonized and oppressed people, through comparisons of mothering in the different communities, are played out through the narrative in what Sally Ledger has identified as a problematic representation of a 'transcultural notion of motherhood'.[25]

Maternal agency subordinated to the state was integral to eugenic rhetoric, which addressed women as mothers of and for the nation. Through her relationship with Karl Pearson, a professor of applied mathematics at University College London, socialist and leading proponent of eugenics, Schreiner developed her investment in eugenic ideologies. In 1888 in his essay 'Woman and Labour', Pearson considered how the (middle-class) woman 'can do freely what she alone can do for society, and yet have full power to control her own special activities, and develop her own individual life'; he found the answer to the woman problem did not lie in the 'equality of opportunity' demanded by the women's movement, but in 'special protection, in the socialisation of the State. The woman of the near future will be as thorough a socialist as she is now an out-and-out individualist.'[26] In 'The Woman's Question', Pearson explained that socialism for a woman would mean seeing her subjection to men as being for the good of 'race' progress: 'she has learnt self-control in the past by subjecting her will to his, so in the future she may be able to submit her liberty to the restraints demanded by social welfare, and to submit to the conditions imposed by race-permanence.'[27]

Schreiner's responses to Pearson's ideas were developed in an essay, 'The Woman Question' of 1899, and her own vision of motherhood expressed in her influential work, *Woman and Labour* (1911), taken up by the suffragettes in the early twentieth century. It is permeated with the eugenicist and imperialist values and ideas of racial supremacy. Her thesis contends that in modern, industrialized societies, advances in technology and machinery have so transformed material conditions that relations of inequality between the sexes have flourished. Whilst men's field of labour has expanded and become more specialized, 'civilized' (white European) women's traditional domestic and agricultural roles have been usurped, but their development has not kept pace with that of men's. Falling birth rates, coupled with children being brought up by paid carers and educators, mean that such women have degenerated into *'sex-parasitism'* (*WL* 77): financially dependent, they subsist on their male hosts.

Schreiner sees evolution through a Lamarckian lens (unlike Pearson), and claims that mothers literally pass on their attenuated form and functions to the race, in turn producing an effete and weak offspring. Thus the nation stagnates, and the progress of the Northern race is arrested. In order to reverse this degenerationist trend, Schreiner insists that women need the opportunity to fulfil themselves in the workplace, and the full education and training to enable them to do it. However, she does not comment on how childcare would be managed, despite the considerable debate on communitarian models of child-raising developed through the period since the Owenite social-ism of the 1830s. Schreiner argues that although Western women's attributes have atrophied, they can be developed again and transmitted to the next generation.

Unlike many others in the women's movement, Schreiner's analysis recognizes class: significantly, she points out that the basis of men's theory 'Let Woman be content to be the "Divine Child-bearer" and ask no more' (*WL* 200) is predicated on the labour of women of the working classes, remarking that '[i]t is not the labour, or the amount of labour, so much as the amount of reward that interferes with his ideal of the eternal womanly' (*WL* 204). Where her argument, crucially, hinges on eugenicist principles is in the text's concluding demand for this 'not for herself, but in the service of the whole race' (*WL* 128). She describes the Teutonic race of women as the powerful and 'virile' archetypal womanhood, as the touchstone for this future and at the vanguard of the progress of the (white) 'race'.

Schreiner's use of biblical language and allegory was dramatically successful in conveying a notion of a powerful, essential and eternal womanhood. But as Sally Ledger has argued, when Schreiner uses sociobiological, discursive strategies on 'race' she is 'radically attenuating her political vision'.[28] The eloquent plea of *Woman and Labour* for equal rights to labour and an independent living became a demand central to the second-wave feminist movement, but the text's underpinning eugenic ideology of racial purity and power is a troubling one to today's feminists.

A popular writer, whose plots link maternal instinct with race motherhood in relation to Empire at the height of the New Woman novel, was 'Iota', pseudonym of Kathleen Mannington Caffyn. Although she has been identified as a New Woman writer both to her contemporaries[29] and in recent scholarship,[30] her status as a *feminist* New Woman writer is doubtful. Iota's novels ultimately reinforce traditional norms of feminine aspiration – marriage and motherhood as vehicles to reverse degenerationist trends of godlessness and emasculation, and actively oppose careers for women. Although many feminists, such as Schreiner, shared her belief in the primacy of motherhood for women, Caffyn, who styled herself 'not a literary woman, nothing of a bluestocking',[31] unlike Schreiner, presented intellectualism and femininity as mutually exclusive.

Caffyn clearly emphasized the political differences of her novel, *A Yellow Aster* (1894), from Olive Schreiner's (who had refused her editor's request to amend the ending of *The Story of An African Farm* with Lyndall's marriage). In an interview with Caffyn in *Shafts*, despite praise for that novel she commented that '[Schreiner's] ideas about marriage are very advanced and modern, and I agree with them only to a certain extent . . . I am not an advanced woman. I do not believe in "woman's rights".'[32] Whilst its title alerted and enticed readers with its nod toward the notorious *Yellow Book*, and connotations of deviant sexuality in its metaphor for unnatural femininity, *A Yellow Aster* was ultimately conservative in its moral. In common with other New Woman feminist texts, the novel contains an indictment of the ignorance in which girls are kept of the responsibilities and duties of sexual relations in marriage, but it is essentially an anti-New Woman novel which defines femininity as maternity.

A Yellow Aster's representation of a dysfunctional family and subsequent failure of the marriage of the protagonist Gwen Waring, reproduces the dichotomy of reason and emotion which was a staple of earlier Victorian values. Gwen's intellectual and atheist parents are too involved in pondering mathematical problems and scientific research to care for and nurture Gwen and her brother. Gwen is the 'yellow aster' who fails to develop empathy or tender feelings; she thus enters in to her own marriage as an 'experiment' with a man she does not love and suffers the humiliation of submitting to marital 'duties' and the resulting pregnancy. Caffyn condemns the loveless marriage on ethical, religious grounds, but fails to point to the material constraints upon women which necessitate it, instead laying the blame for girls' ignorance at the door of women who have chosen a career or education over domestic and family duty. In Gwen, Caffyn said she was portraying an 'unnatural' woman; the result of conflict between the generations of mother and daughter: '[i]f we get so exceedingly intellectual there is a great danger of neglectful absorption. There is undoubtedly a want of sympathy between mothers and daughters. The "Revolt of the Daughters" shows that. "Gwen" of course, was the outcome of unnatural conditions.'[33]

Caffyn's views on motherhood are 'New' in the eugenicist values of a colonial perspective on the need for girls to be able to procure the fittest of British men for marriage. In *A Comedy in Spasms* (1895) Caffyn, who had herself lived in Australia, used the environment of the colony and the passage of emigration in order to explore race motherhood and the social confines which impede it. Elizabeth Marrable, a colonial, represents the 'New Girl' who will regenerate England with her healthier body, freer, enterprising 'Prospector' manners and maternal instincts generated by the hot sun and clean air of the Australian bush. Following her father's bankruptcy and death, she emigrates 'home' with her family, but on board ship falls in love with Tom Temple, a man who is already engaged.

Caffyn deplores the way in which the making of eugenically fit matches is impeded by the social and class conventions of marriage arrangements; observing the flirtatious activities of Miss Marrable, fellow traveller Miss Sefton demands to know 'what that fraud Selection is pottering after, that he can't chip in and clinch matters' (CS 112). Moral codes of femininity (restraint, propriety, sexual passivity) are under strain from the instinct for maternity with which sexuality is fused in the aroused Elizabeth.

In common with social purity narratives, the novel articulates anxieties about the current degenerative state of masculinity, and the romance plot presents three types of manhood from which Elizabeth must select the most fit. Her first suitor, Count Ferdinand Fitz-Clarence Falconer, although suitably moneyed, is a decadent figure who has supersensitive nerves and poor eyesight, an over-fondness for 'china shepherdesses', 'rose draped boudoirs with soft scented air', and an Aesthete's aversion to 'bright green' (CS 23) – corrupt tendencies which a discerning Elizabeth regrets would not have belonged to his Crusader descendants. It is the handsome, sporting Tom Temple, a 'Thor come down among us with a boy's face' (CS 88) whose physique marks him out as a favoured contender for sexual selection. Yet her marriage is made with the distinctly dysgenic – a short and 'yellow skinned' 'spindle shanks' – but wealthy, Colonel Prynne, a man she does not love, but must marry to restore the family's fortunes (CS 101). Prynne and Elizabeth marry, and the story ends with her unhappy and childless. Whilst A Yellow Aster is acerbic and pointed in its critique of women's sexual ignorance, the more light-hearted, comic approach of A Comedy in Spasms lacks the proselytizing edge of, for example, Grand's moral purity. But the endings of Caffyn's novels proscribe not only that women remain within the hegemonic structures of womanhood, but reinforce that these offer women their ultimate and fulfilling purpose.

The sexuality of the colonial New Woman was also of interest to Victoria Cross but with very different inflections of gender and race politics which sometimes addressed the subject of 'interracial' marriage. Her best-selling novel *Anna Lombard* (1901), set in India, sees the eponymous New Woman protagonist ultimately elevated to the status of a heroine of Empire, whose act of infanticide restores the sovereignty of white imperialism. Along the way however, we witness the expression of a powerful female sexuality in an ambiguous portrayal of a secret marriage between the Colonel's daughter, Anna, and her Pathan servant, Gaida Khan. After Gaida's death from cholera, and having conceived a child with him, she marries her first love, a white colonial civil servant, Gerald Etheridge. After the birth of her baby, Anna reasons that the infant will drive the couple apart, and chooses to suffocate him to death. Like other of Cross's fiction, such as *The Woman Who Didn't* (1895), this cautionary tale highlights the dangers of repression of sexuality and late marriage, and reaches a highly reactionary and disturbing conclusion in a couple happily united by infanticide.

The infanticide plot violently enacts eugenic imperatives for racial purity in the context of empire-building.[34] By the end of the century fears about the control over British India were concerned not only with governmental and military administrations, in which Anglo-Indians were a small minority of the population, but as Nancy Paxton has noted, with the interracial mixture of the population and the way in which this might blur boundaries of colonial identity and racial hierarchies.[35]

Identification of Anna with a powerful but decadent femininity is made through the historical figure of Catherine Sforza, a notorious fifteenth-century noblewoman of the Medici family who was a poisoner. Early on, a masquerade costume party is organized by Gerald in order to satisfy his fantasy of seeing Anna dress-up to resemble Sforza. The masquerade prefigures Anna's act of infanticide, establishing an ideological frame for the reader with which to interpret Anna's action. The pointed comparison elevates her into an unusual turn of the century *femme fatale*: a mythical, heroic, rather than a degenerate figure.[36] The identification made between a modern woman and a *femme*

fatale of the Renaissance and the Middle Ages was also significant in Vernon Lee's writing to explore and historicize female
sexuality, as discussed later in this chapter. Female agency, as
motherhood, is measured in the supreme act of love which
breaks the laws of Nature; for Anna to kill her baby is to 'erase'
the betrayal of colonial hegemony it represents, apparent in its
'dusky tint' (*AL* 291).

Shoshana Milgram Knapp finds that the depiction of love in
Cross's fiction is one 'transcending boundaries of race, religion,
culture and legal sanction',[37] yet those border crossings which
recur in Cross's fiction, generate unease not only for today's
reader (for example in the fantasies of sexual violence concerning Anna and Gaida) but for Cross, who seeks to contain what
she has suggested. In *Anna Lombard*, Anna's violent act is a
rejection of the 'natural laws' of motherhood and mother-love
which, like Jessamine's in *A Superfluous Woman*, can be read as
an expression of a quintessentially modern female agency. If as
Josephine McDonagh suggests of the Victorian period, 'motherhood had come to symbolize civilization itself, and infanticide
represents its boundaries',[38] Anna's act of child murder determines what kind of woman she wants to be in order to
contribute to a modern civilization with a eugenic future.

The short story was a modern form in the 1890s. The brevity
of the form coincided with the rise of a print culture which saw
the demise of the circulating libraries and the three-decker novel
of the mid Victorian period, and the rise of distribution networks
such as the newsstand and the railway station, and increased use
of advertising by publishers. The form also lent itself practically
and economically to making a living for some women, particularly if literary work must be combined with motherhood; the
new periodical and magazine publication industry created a
receptive and competitive market where women might sell their
labour for a monthly subsistence, as did the fictional Marion
Yule in Gissing's *New Grub Street*, or Cosima Chudleigh in
Paston's *A Writer of Books*.

This relatively new form enabled experimentation with narrative structures and a break with the conventions of the
old literary realism, the domestic novel and the romance.
The modern short story was characterized by enquiry and
did not necessarily seek a conclusion or resolution; the enigma,

ambiguity and fragment, all tended to convey the uncertainties and ideological interrogations of the *fin de siècle*. Short stories by George Egerton, Victoria Cross, Vernon Lee and Ella D'Arcy all use aspects of the fantastic, myth and the form of allegory to explore sexuality and gender relations.

John Lane and Elkin Matthews's quarterly book-length magazine, the *Yellow Book* (thirteen issues from April 1894 to April 1897), with literary editor Henry Harland, and Aubrey Beardsley as its art editor, quickly became a notorious volume associated with decadent art; it featured new work by women, most of whom were not well known for their fiction, and had a female assistant editor, Ella D'Arcy whose stories featured in nearly every issue.[39] Victoria Cross's early short story 'Theodora: A Fragment' appeared in the *Yellow Book* (v) in 1895. She would go on to develop the fragment into a full length novel in *Six Chapters of a Man's Life* (1903). Cross's conception of Theodora Dudley, presented by the narrator, Cecil Ray, is of a woman who challenges gender conventions, what Shoshana Milgram Knapp has called the figure of 'the revolutionary androgyne',[40] and the narrative is of ambivalent stance on sexual morality. Like the typical New Woman, of a confident and confidential manner, Theodora has 'an intellectual but careless and independent spirit', which we are invited to relate to her economic independence. She arouses Ray's social, sexual and emotional curiosity by 'a dash of virility, a hint at dissipation, a suggestion of a certain decorous looseness of morals and fastness of manners' ('Theodora' 12). Early on, Ray's atypical sexual predilections are hinted at in his remarks to his friend Digby: 'I think I have heard of men remaining celibates before now, especially men with my tastes' ('Theodora' 7), so it is her boyish figure as well as manner, the 'full chin' with a trace of a moustache, 'that curious masculine shade upon the upper lip' (26), that intrigues him. A parallel drawn between her beauty and that of a portrait of a young Sikh man with his head uncovered, emphasizes her difference. In a scene of masquerade evoking an Egyptian bazaar, these crossings of racial and gender identities are emphasized further when Theodora dresses in an Eastern fez hat and tight, silk zouave jacket and smokes a cigarette.[41]

Theodora lacks the usual feminine attractions of the Victorian heroine; her figure has 'little suggestion of the duties or powers of Nature' ('Theodora' 24); she bespeaks 'a poor if possible mother, and a still poorer nurse' ('Theodora' 21). Desire for the beautiful Theodora is configured as an extension of the doctrine of art for art's sake to pleasure for its own sake, in which sexuality is divorced – even liberated – from Nature and its use-value, maternity. Separating pleasure and desire from eugenic ends, the (male) narrator opines that the 'sharpest, most violent, stimulus we may say, the true essence of pleasure, lies in some gratification which has no claim, whatever, in any sense, to be beneficial or useful, or to have any ulterior motive, conscious or instinctive or any lasting result, or any fulfilment of any object but which is simple gratification and dies naturally in its own excess' ('Theodora' 20). The fragmentary form of the narrative condones the sexually assertive behaviour of its androgynous protagonist Theodora, for the story has an open ending, abruptly finishing on a passionate kiss between the two acquaintances, without authorial recrimination or resolution.

Lane published George Egerton's *Keynotes* in 1893 and *Discords* a year later, heading up what would become his new series, 'Keynotes', bringing Egerton fame and notoriety. Beardsley's illustration for her Keynotes collection typified the decadent in turn of the century culture. Amongst the critical responses, Owen Seaman in *Punch* parodied 'The Cross Line' as 'She Notes' by 'Borgia Smudgiton';[42] Hugh Stutfield writing on the new 'degenerate' fiction in *Blackwood's Magazine* made particular reference to *Discords*, deplored its 'erotomania' and introspective characters who 'when they are not talking of psychology, they are discussing physiology. They search for new thrills and sensations, and they possess a maddening faculty of dissecting and probing their "primary impulses" – especially the sexual ones.'[43] Critics have credited Egerton with innovating modern literary aesthetics and techniques, and anticipating the ideas of French feminist *écriture féminine*: her writing is characterized by fantasy, impressionism, the description of psychological states and moods, and truncated, open-ended narratives. In conveying a peculiarly feminine, 'witch-like' sensibility, Egerton's prose centres on intuitions and moments of understanding: a sense of immediacy is conveyed by the use of the present tense. The stories focus on a woman's sense of self, a consciousness that is inextricable from her sexuality and physicality.

Egerton read and relished the candour of Scandinavian naturalism, including the works of Henrik Ibsen, August Strindberg, Bjørnstjerne Bjørnsen, and Knut Hamsun whose novel *Hunger* she translated into English in 1890, and their subject matter and style informed her own. Egerton denied any affiliation with the New Woman movement, yet she wrote about the concerns of contemporary feminism; disturbing depictions of domestic and sexual violence ('Wedlock', 'Gone Under', 'Virgin Soil'), alcoholism ('A Shadow's Slant', 'Under Northern Sky'), poverty, and prostitution characterize Egerton's treatment of the conditions of married life in which both working- and middle-class women are vulnerable to economic, physical and psychological abuse. Whilst examining the material conditions of women's lives, Egerton also develops a cosmological viewpoint of women that, in common with social purity feminists like Ellice Hopkins and Frances Swiney, posits an essential female nature of moral superiority. However, her vision of the true nature of womanhood departed radically in fundamental ways from these contemporaries. Like them, she criticized male sexual hypocrisy and asserted women's right to make marital and sexual choices, but she also celebrated women who could take pleasure in sexual experience and power and aestheticized their experience ('A Cross Line', 'A Little Grey Glove') and explored their need for fulfilment, insisting upon a unique female imaginary and capacity for erotic fantasy, although this model of sexuality still corresponded to a heterosexual one.

In 'The Regeneration of Two' a woodland lakeside is the natural setting for an impassioned emotional and intellectual encounter between a male stranger and female protagonist; in response to his criticism of the artificial manners of women she replies:

> We have been taught to shrink from the honest expression of our wants and feelings as violations of modesty, or at least good taste. We are always battling with some bottom layer of real womanhood that we may not reveal; the primary impulses of our original destiny keep shooting out mimosa-like threads of natural feeling through the husk of our artificial selves, producing complex creatures. (*Keynotes and Discords* 198)

Part of this identity of 'real womanhood' was a sexual maternity in which the woman chooses a fit mate, and features in many of these stories ('Gone Under', 'The Spell of the White Elf', 'A Cross Line'). In 'A Cross Line' the heroine fantasizes herself riding wildly on a horse, and dancing before an admiring and desirous male crowd, 'hundreds of faces' gazing at her dressed in a 'cobweb garment of wondrous tissue'. Her sexual power and potency – registered further when she recognizes her pregnant state – is depicted in her performance: 'she stands with out-stretched arms and passion-filled eyes, poised on one slender foot, asking a supreme note to finish her dream of motion' (*Keynotes and Discords* 20). Ledger has emphasized how 'the "dream of motion" suggests the cadences of sexual arousal' and the way in which the imagery here points toward 'an autoerotic fantasy of sexual congress'.[44]

Egerton reified a female essentialism: 'the primitive, the generic, that makes her sacred, mystic, to the best men' (*Keynotes and Discords* 197) which she saw as repressed by the confines of polite urban society and its Victorian mores; these deterministic characteristics of Egerton's vision have been described by Ann Heilmann as 'strident inconsistencies' which she argues 'point to the instability of New Woman discourses whose subversive impetus and reformist vision were all too often clogged by essentialism'.[45] Yet despite Egerton's seemingly ideological con-tradictions, her imaginary was a unique one which conveyed optimism and hope. For example 'The Regeneration of Two' which concludes with a successful commune of working single mothers, and a partnership between a New Woman and a New Man based on interdependence, respect and equality: one of the very few 'free love unions' to be portrayed as hopeful of success in women's writing at this time. Egerton's attention to the relationship between the self and language, its role in construct-ing experience rather than just expressing it, has a resemblance to an aestheticist perspective pursued by Vernon Lee.

Lee is identified by critics today as a 'female aesthete' and a 'decadent woman', and by her own admission she avoided the Woman Question;[46] but her writing does engage with feminist concerns over gender ideologies, albeit in an allegorical way, and therefore makes an instructive comparison with the polemics of her New Woman peers. Her interests in purity, her critique of art for art's sake and exposition of decadence and the 'fleshly school', yet her friendship and admiration for Walter Pater,

Oscar Wilde and others of the aesthete circle meant she had a complex critical and personal relationship with those debates. Educated beyond the means of some of her female contemporaries and with an independent income, Lee had a lifestyle which enabled her to write at a more leisurely pace and, to an extent, to choose the 'high-brow' periodicals in which she wished to publish. She developed self-consciously modern methodological and critical affiliations, wit and formal complexity in her successful ghost stories.

Referring in a diary entry to her novel *Miss Brown* (1884), Lee examined 'this seemingly scientific, philanthropic, idealising, decidedly noble-looking nature of mine' and wondered whether 'I [may] be indulging a mere depraved appetite for the loathsome while I *fancy* that I am studying diseases and probing wounds for the sake of diminishing both? Perhaps ... [t]he question is, which of these two, the prudes or the easy-goers, are themselves normal, healthy?'[47] This discourse of the role of writer as a sort of public health officer was shared with social-purity women novelists as a commentary on the unhealthy, sexually immoral texts of male artists. But, Lee asks, how might such a position articulate an interest in the very thing it appears to repudiate?[48] And can perversity infect the examiner who is in the supposedly objective position of 'probing' another's body/text? Lee's self-reflexiveness indicates how her narratives cannot solely be grouped with those of the purity polemics of New Woman writing, and this ambivalence is most clearly situated in her fantasy writing.

Her fairytale story 'Prince Alberic and the Snake Lady' was published in the *Yellow Book*; she also published two collections of stories, *Hauntings: Fantastic Stories* (1890) and *Vanitas: Polite Stories* (1892) which depart from the realism and naturalism of many of the short stories written by women at this time. Vernon Lee's writing on art and literary history was resistant to the prevailing model of criticism in the nineteenth century best represented by John Ruskin and Matthew Arnold. As recent scholarship has argued,[49] Lee consciously signalled her modernity through the shift away from the ideological securities of a Victorian visual economy in aesthetics in which sight was the authoritative sense for critic and artist, and the means of knowing the object, and drew attention to the role of individuals and their internal world in the act of perception. Her emphasis on experiential, embodied perspectives can be identified with Pater, and his decadent aesthetic.[50] The erotic and gothic spirit of androgynous beauty in Pater's *The Renaissance, Studies in Art and Poetry* (1873) informs Vernon Lee's constructions of her ghostly female protagonists in the supernatural stories of obsessive desire in *Hauntings*, including 'Oke of Okehurst', 'Amour Dure' and 'Dionea'.[51]

The uses of myth in these stories undermine contemporary cultural orthodoxies on women's role, and the identity of 'the feminine'. Each story has an image or representation at its centre and variously presents the role of the male gaze in the construction of the feminine subject. Often told from a limited and subjective point of view, such as in letters and diaries, the reader must question which events are real, and which imagined.

The characteristically androgynous spectre of Lee's ghost stories may, in its 'perversity', be read as a configuring of the lesbian. Writing of the literary history of lesbianism, Terry Castle has connected spectrality with a lesbian aesthetic in fiction which delights in the confounding of 'phantasmatic' with 'real'.[52] States of displacement, alterity, estrangement are typically the 'real' for the female subject of lesbian fiction because these states describe subject positions outside the normative roles of a patriarchal and heterosexual order. Thus the real becomes, through a number of stylistic effects, typically formalized in the fantastic spectre, and a ghostly world distorted and estranged in a phantasmagoric way. Although Lee's stories do not ostensibly depict female to female desire – indeed, the ghosts are often male – they nonetheless express an androgynous eroticism which evades, challenges or destroys the male gaze and its controlling sexual economy, so that we might read some of the phantasmic encounters in *Hauntings* as a sort of displacement of lesbianism.

In 'Dionea', historicism – in this case, Hellenism – is used to question the morality of the present, and myth is presented as a cultural repository for that which is absent or repressed from the modern condition. The retelling of the myth of Pygmalion was popular during the end of the nineteenth century, depicting as it did the triumph of Nature over Culture.[53] In 'Dionea', Vernon Lee uses the myth to criticize the notion of the Ideal in beauty and analyse the role of the masculine gaze in constituting the female subject as commodity, a critical exposition which echoes the morals of New Woman social purists. The letters of a physician living on Cyprus tell of the adoption into the island community of a fugitive child washed up from the sea, whom they name Dionea, believing her to be shipwrecked from a Greek ship. The ship-wrecked fugitive Dionea (as Dione the Titan mother of Aphrodite, associated with rose, myrtle and doves) is a magical and mythical figure whose spell of Hellenism, a spirit of passionate and erotic love, disrupts the local community. Dionea is also described with snake imagery, linked to the power of her sexuality and magic, that which exists and extends its potency beyond social, patriarchal confines. The love potions she makes produce disruptive forces, they undo social conventions; matches made by families for convenience are rebelled against. Equally, true loves are broken and renegade nuns run off to sea with sailors.

When a sculptor, Waldemar, with his wife Gertrude, set up a studio in the village on the old site of the temple of Venus, the now adult Dionea poses as his model for a statue of the goddess Venus. Coming under Dionea's thrall the sculptor has to realize defeat and admit that the living, natural woman is more beautiful than his art can make her: the male creator's representation cannot contain her. 'Unmanned' he attacks the statue's face in a gesture of sexual violence: destruction follows. The cliff top studio is discovered burnt to the ground, Gertrude's dead body on an altar, and the sculptor's on the shore below. Dionea has vanished, and is later sighted at the prow of a Greek ship sailing out to sea.

In the triangular relationship, Lee examines women's collusion in the 'virgin/ whore' dichotomy so dear to male aestheticists and artists. Gertrude seeks to maintain the image of her own purity through sacrificing other women to her husband's desires; in a startling image the narrator presents Gertrude that 'snow white saint' as a 'pale, demure diaphanous creature not the more earthly for approaching motherhood, scanning the girls of our village with the eyes of a slave dealer'(*Hauntings* 90). By looking for a girl whom her husband can gaze on and, by implication, have sexual congress with, she preserves her own identity as 'soul-ful'. The authorial condemnation of this sexual economy participates in the view of social-purity feminists of the hypocrisy of the middle-class marriage contracted in the market place, and the cultural feminine ideal as the Madonna – ethereal, disembodied yet simultaneously maternal.

The fantastic opens up a space between the terms of morality, purity and perversity and what is beautiful in the culture; in Lee's work, this enables a more complex and ambiguous conception of the relationship between the artist, the work and the reader/spectator, than the conclusive moral certainties which characterize didactic writers like Grand. Yet writers as diametrically opposed as Grand and Lee both satirized male aestheticism whilst drawing on its stylistic qualities to present feminist critiques.

Although clear ideological positions and identifications with certain political campaigns can be identified, the dynamics of their interaction with other literary movements and aesthetic agendas of the period do not allow a unified or consistent subjectivity for the New Woman writer to be posited. A meeting reported by the *Woman's Signal* in 1894 of the Fifth Annual Meeting of the Co-fraternity of Women Writers which took place at the Criterion Restaurant in London makes this point. A seating plan illustrated how aestheticist and New Woman Mona Caird was seated at a dinner table with journalist Evelyn March-Phillips; the essayist Alice Meynell with the polemic novelist Mrs Mannington Caffyn; and the best-seller writer of military romances John Strange Winter with the aesthetic poet Elizabeth Sharp.[54] We can only imagine the conversations and disputes which took place, but the evidence of such meetings reminds us of the affiliations existing in the professional networks and social circles in which women writers moved in their lives. The era of the New Woman extends beyond the nineteenth century well into the twentieth; the figure continued to be reflected in the prose and political life of the Edwardian age, particularly as regards the theatre, as we see in the following chapter.

4

New Woman Drama

In 1911, Elizabeth Robins made a speech to the Women Writers' Suffrage League in which she acclaimed what she called 'the Real Girl', not a type imagined by men, but a 'creature of infinite variety, of curiosities and ambitions, of joy in physical action, of high dreams of love and service'. The task of the women writers was to represent her: 'The Great Adventure is before her. *Your* great adventure is to report her faithfully. So that her children's children reading her story shall be lifted up – proud and full of hope. "Of such stuff", they shall say, "our mothers were! Sweethearts and wives – yes, and other things besides: leaders, discoverers, militants, fighting every form of wrong." '[1]

By 1911, the New Woman has become the Real Girl and New Woman drama has become suffrage drama. The battle has not been won but it has shifted ground and has a clearer focus. The shift had been signalled by Elizabeth Robins's play *Votes for Women!* which was first performed at the Royal Court Theatre in April 1907. Robins's play lies outside the time span this book has allotted to novels by New Woman writers but in the case of drama the period has to be extended because some of the most interesting material belongs to the Edwardian theatre. New Woman drama was slow to begin; Elizabeth Robins's play represents a realization of what it had been struggling towards. To omit it and some of the plays that came after it would be to leave the story unfinished.

The story begins with a very different kind of play, *The New Woman: An Original Comedy in Four Acts* by Sidney Grundy, first performed at the Comedy Theatre in that crucial year for New Women, 1894. Grundy was a prolific dramatist, producing numerous farces and melodramas, generally popular enough to earn him a good living and a regular presence on the West End stage. *The New Woman* uses many of the features of melodrama – the overheard conversation, for instance, which results in a climax to the plot – and is peopled with stock characters from drawing-room comedy: the pompous colonel, the grand, aristocratic lady, a supercilious servant, a clutch of young women talking about marriage. But in this case, the young women are the smoking, outspoken, mannish stereotypes of the New Woman and their conversation is in favour of the independence of women and against conventional marriage. One of their number is a doctor, who sums up the writing achievements of the group: 'the day of awakening has come. Sylvester, in her *Aspirations after a Higher Morality*, Bethune, in her *Man, the Betrayer*, Vivash, in her *Foolish Virgins*, have postulated the sexual problem from every imaginable point of view; and I myself have contributed to the discussion a modest little treatise . . . *Naked and Unashamed*.'[2] In case the audience has not grasped the point, Lady Wargave says, 'Excuse my ignorance, but I have been away from England for so many years. Can this be the New Woman I have read about?'

The main plot concerns two married couples, the Sylvesters and the Cazanoves. Mr Cazanove and Mrs Sylvester are writing a book together on the ethics of marriage, and both neglect their spouses in doing so. Margery Cazanove, who has been Lady Wargrave's maid before her marriage, is described as 'a woman! That's all Margery is!' It takes the length of the play for her to show her devotion to her husband, in spite of his ill treatment of her, and for him to realize her worth: 'I want you to be nothing less or more – only a woman', he says to her in the closing lines of the play. The Sylvesters are sent to try to patch up their marriage, with the cynical realization that Mrs Sylvester was only ever after the ordinary female success of a relationship with a man. As Margery says to her: 'You call yourself a New Woman – you're not New at all. You're just as old as Eve . . . You only want one thing – the one thing every woman wants – the one thing that no woman's life's worth living without! A true man's love!' This very conservative play endorses conventional marriage, upholds the double standard, places women in a subservient, supporting role, and condemns higher learning for them. A rather uneasy comedy, its targets for humour are principally the New Women, who are wheeled on at intervals to appear strident or foolish. They cannot even light the right end of a cigarette. In line with the whole drift of the play, in the final scene one of the New Women appears to be going to marry the colonel, an old *roué* many years her senior.

Grundy's play shares some characteristics with Wilde's comedies, but Wilde's spirited young women and forceful older women offer a more positive and subversive view of changes in modern women's attitudes and behaviour than any thing Grundy has to offer. 'The home seems to me to be the proper sphere for the man', says Gwendolen in *The Importance of Being Earnest*. 'Once a man begins to neglect his domestic duties he becomes painfully effeminate, does he not?' Male dramatists during the last two decades of the nineteenth century seem to have been more alert to both the threat and the promise of the New Woman. George Bernard Shaw's Vivie Warren in *Mrs Warren's Profession* (1894), his St Joan, or Dolly in *You Never Can Tell* (1897) are all New Women of a kind, although Shaw is unable to allow his heroines to exert their independence to become other than good wives, a force of nature, religious fanatics or hardened shrews like Vivie.

The most powerful of the dramatists of this period in addressing the woman question was, of course, Henrik Ibsen. In the figure of Nora in *A Doll's House* (1879) he embodied the unsatisfied wife who leaves husband and child for an impoverished but independent life. 'I believe that first and foremost I am an individual', says Nora. 'I'm not content any more with what people say or what it says in books. I have to think things out for myself, and get things clear' (Act 3). In *Hedda Gabler* (1890) Ibsen presented the destructive force of a woman whose energies and lust for power are frustrated by the limitations of bourgeois marriage. 'I've often thought there's only one thing in the world I'm any good at ... Boring myself to death. So now you know', Hedda says in Act 2 of the play, and the decisive factor in urging her towards suicide is to find herself in the power of another person: 'Subject to your will and your demands. No longer free! ... That's a thought that I'll never endure! Never' (Act 4).

Ibsen's plays began to be produced in London in the late 1880s and early 1890s, with *A Doll's House* in 1889 at the Novelty Theatre, arousing immediate controversy. Elizabeth Robins, along with Marion Lea, produced *Hedda Gabler* at the Vaudeville Theatre in 1891, with Robins playing the part of Hedda. Prejudice against Ibsen meant that she had no backer for the play and had to borrow against her own possessions to produce it. The play was viewed as outrageous, a study in psychopathology, and a picture of a 'monstrous specimen' of womanhood which warned of the extremes to which New Women might go. Max Nordau's attack on Ibsen in *Degeneration* saw Ibsen's women as the most serious symptom of the decline of civilization, as sick, deranged, ego-maniacs, with no true regard for their natural destiny as wives and mothers. But to the feminists of the period, Ibsen was a rallying force, performances of his plays eagerly attended by the more radical of their number, and, as in the case of Eleanor Marx, translated into English.[3] In *Daughters of Decadence* Elaine Showalter quotes (p. vii) Edith Lees's description of the reaction of women, including Olive Schreiner and Eleanor Marx, to the first performance of *A Doll's House* in 1889:

> We were restive and impetuous and almost savage in our arguments. This was either the end of the world or the beginning of a new world for women. What did it mean? Was there hope or despair in the banging of that door? Was it life or death for women? Was it joy or sorrow for men? Was it revelation or disaster?

Plays about New Women by male dramatists followed in Ibsen's wake, one of the most successful being Arthur Pinero's *The Notorious Mrs Ebbsmith*, staged in March 1895 at the Garrick Theatre. Pinero was sometimes called 'the English Ibsen' because his subject matter was often controversial and his approach naturalistic. Agnes Ebbsmith is an unconventional woman who despises femininity and marriage and has a free union with a married man. Together they will educate the world in what true love, socialist principles and high-mindedness mean. But her man, Lucas Cleeve, is weak and cannot sustain the high ideals she has; he also is unprepared for sexual abstinence. Afraid of losing him she turns to sexual seductiveness, and eventually gives him back to his wife. She is a very contradictory figure: sweet-voiced and gentle in private, and a shrill propagandist in public; self-sacrificing although clear about Lucas Cleeve's failings; an atheist but capitulates to the Bible in the end. William Archer said that 'her spiritual history does not hang together. It is not probably constructed or possibly expressed.' Mrs Campbell, who played her, said that 'she was a new and daring type, the woman agitator, the pessimist with original independent ideas.' Lucas Cleeve is a neurasthenic male, and the 'felt shallowness of his nature suggests the generally barren and inadequate nature of contemporary society'.[4]

Pinero does not have the courage to give Agnes any future. Having failed in an ideal relationship (reminiscent of both George Gissing's *The Odd Women* and Grant Allen's *The Woman Who Did*) she has no prospects other than life in a dreary country parsonage, and is a beaten woman. She is a New Woman who can't live up to her ambitions, and is betrayed by her femaleness: 'my sex has found me out.'[5] Though not a comedy, *The Notorious Mrs Ebbsworth* has much in common with Grundy's play; both give a platform to the New Woman and her ideas but she is shown as incapable of carrying them through because in doing so she is acting against her woman's nature.

By the turn of the century, the portrayal of the New Woman by male dramatists has taken a more positive turn. *The Last of the De Mullins: A Play without a Preface* by Sir John Hankin, first staged at the Haymarket Theatre in December 1908, endorses independence for women, but the justifying force in this is maternal pride. The old family of the De Mullins, acutely aware of their respectability, have two daughters, Agnes who remains miserably at home, and Janet who has left to have an illegitimate child. The illness of the father precipitates a visit from Janet, accompanied by her son, now aged about 6. During the play it emerges who the boy's father is; on meeting him Janet refuses to marry him.

Mr De Mullin wants Janet to return home so that her son can be the next generation of De Mullins, but this would mean that Janet would have to give up her independence as the owner of a successful hat shop, and this she refuses to do. De Mullin tries to compel her but she laughs in his face and leaves, with her son, the last of the De Mullins. Agnes, in the mean time, has lost her chance of marriage because of the narrowness of her family's views (particularly their dislike of 'trade') and her own timidity.

The play demonstrates the waning power of fathers over daughters, the imperative towards motherhood, with or without the support of a father for the child, and the foolish snobbery of the declining upper classes. The play keeps its focus in view, moves swiftly along and though not subtle in characterization, uses types effectively. Janet is unmistakably a New Woman: she earns her own living, she has exercised sexual freedom, and she defies established norms. She is also a cyclist, the bicycle being both sign of and vehicle for the New Woman, and possibly the cause of her 'downfall': 'I never approved of Janet's bicycling you remember, Jane', says De Mullin's stuffy sister. The trend of the failed New Woman, whose descent into conventional femininity or neurosis has been the theme of earlier dramas, has been halted in this play.

But in the last decades of the nineteenth century, the mental instability or general foolishness of the New Woman characters were prevailing features in the plays of the period. And if the female characters were abnormal, the actresses who played them were viewed as especially vulnerable to derangement. Kerry Powell has suggested that the link between women, madness and monstrosity on the stage was so pervasive in this period 'as to constitute a discernable cultural pattern'.[6] Powell cites the title character in George Moore's *A Mummer's Wife* (1885) who descends into violence, disease, madness, deformity and finally death because of her career on the stage. Sybil Vane in Wilde's *The Picture of Dorian Gray* is depicted as no more than the parts she plays, devoid of selfhood, ruined as an actress and a woman when her love for Dorian awakens her to real emotion: 'The girl never really lived, and so she has never really died', says Lord Henry. 'Mourn for Ophelia if you like. Put ashes on your head because Cordelia was strangled ... But don't waste your tears on Sybil Vane. She was less real than they are' (Ch. 8). The Victorian tendency to see the actress as demonically or inhumanly possessed by her art had been earlier illustrated in the figure of Vashti (modelled on the actress Rachel) in Charlotte Brontë's *Villette* (1853):

> I found upon her something neither of woman nor of man: in each of her eyes sat a devil. These evil forces bore her through the tragedy ... They wrote HELL on her straight, haughty brow. They tuned her voice to the note of torment ... It was a marvellous sight: a mighty revelation. It was a spectacle low, horrible, immoral. (Ch. 23)

Brontë saw the Jewish Rachel in London in 1851, and her sense of the peril of the stage and of her own daring in witnessing the denatured force of the actress is metaphorically conveyed in the fire which consumes the theatre. But her response was also one of liberating excitement, a 'mighty revelation' to witness a woman in commanding public display, an occasion 'marked in my book of life, not with white, but with a deep-red cross'.

In George Eliot's *Daniel Deronda* (1876), when Daniel finally meets his mother, a great singer and actress, who has abandoned him at birth, he finds 'her worn beauty had a strangeness in it as if she were not quite a human mother but a Melusina', and she admits that she has 'not felt exactly what other women feel'. Through her the novel makes its feminist cry for the right for women to express their talents and individuality: 'You can never imagine what it is to have a man's force of genius in you, yet to suffer the slavery of being a girl' (Ch. 51). Yet her lonely, embittered death is a warning of the sacrifices such a career forces on a woman, and the implication is that she has made a wrong decision in following it.

The strong suspicion and fear of the place of the stage in women's lives is the background to the relatively slow development of New Woman drama by women. If it took determination and courage, and at times desperation, to become an actress, even more so was the challenge of writing plays, and getting them produced and managed. The dependency of women on male patronage is well illustrated in Constance Fenimore Woolson's short story, 'Miss Grief', in which an impoverished, drab, ageing spinster brings her play to a literary gentleman living a very comfortable life. He condescends to read it and is struck by its passion and originality but he doesn't tell her so, and leaves her to think it is unexceptional. After her death he tidies it up and has it produced as his own, to huge success.[7]

Yet in spite of such discouragement, the stage had offered women a degree of independence from the time of the Restoration, and even for respectable women it had always held an allure. From the seventeenth century women had been managers and occasionally writers as well as actresses but with the Victorian age these opportunities had declined and, as Viv Gardner and Susan Rutherford have said, the theatre became 'a problematic domain': 'In a society which, particularly since the mid-eighteenth century, had excluded its females from public discourse, the theatre was anathema. It not only placed its women on public view but often put them in positions of physical and emotional intimacy with men not their fathers or husbands.'[8]

The history of women playwrights in the nineteenth century before the age of the New Woman is largely a lost one, either because their plays have disappeared from the theatrical canon or because the assumption that women could not write for the stage was so great that they rarely attempted it. As Powell says, 'Much of Victorian drama reduces women nearly to the level of properties – ancillary images imprisoned in male-written texts, shaped and constrained by male interpretations.'[9] But those women who did write for the mid-Victorian stage, like Lucy Clifford, Catherine Crowe, Sara Lane and Clo Graves, often produced strong, even swashbuckling, melodramatic female protagonists in their plays, whose passions and courage were aroused, in true maternal fashion, in defence of their children or other helpless individuals. The 'woman's play' which most conforms to the idea of women's destiny as bound to their maternal function was the adapting for the stage of Mrs Henry Wood's novel, *East Lynne* (1861). In fact there were several adaptations, all, as Powell points out,[10] by male dramatists, in which Isobel Carlyle's conduct as an unworthy mother duly punished for her waywardness, is exaggerated. It was in one of these dramatizations, by T. A. Palmer in 1874, and not in the novel, that Isobel, watching incognito the death of her son, says the famous line, 'Dead! and never called me mother.' As will become clear, the pull of the maternal instinct will be an enduring theme in New Woman drama.

The attempts to raise the status of the theatre in the second half of the century, to divorce serious theatre from music hall and pantomime, helped to create a space in which women's theatre could flourish. The financial gains now possible for both men and women, due to a recently introduced system whereby playwrights received on average 10 per cent of gross takings, was a contributory factor in making the theatre an attractive proposition for earning women. And as Gardner points out,[11] the improvement in the theatre as a career for women had been brought about in no small way by actress-managers such as May Anderson, Florence Farr and Marie Wilton, the last of these borrowing £1,000 from her brother-in-law to transform the

Queen's Theatre from a variety playhouse into a theatre attracting the middle and professional classes, and renaming it the Prince of Wales Theatre. For women to manage a theatre gave opportunities to choose plays and parts which suited them, and also helped to change the culture of the theatre, making it more respectable and attuned to female patronage, opening up a public space for women. This presented a challenge to the male theatrical establishment, as George Bernard Shaw noted in his introduction to William Archer's *The Theatrical 'World' of 1894*: 'the time is ripe for the advent of the actress-manageress, and that we are on the verge of something like a struggle between the sexes for the dominion of the London theatres, a struggle which ... must in the long run end disastrously for the side which is furthest behind the times. And that side is at present the men's side.'[12] But the men's side would not give up the struggle lightly and there was serious opposition from male critics and dramatists to what they considered to be the feminization of the theatre. Ridicule was a favourite weapon, along with attempts to show women engaged as managers or patrons in the theatre as 'unfeminine', as the reception of Madge Kendal's production of Ibsen's *The Pillars of Society* shows:

> Outside the circle doors of the Opera-Comique ... there were assembled some twenty to thirty of these manly women, eager to listen to Ibsen ... The fearful business made by these two dozen members of the superior sex in getting into a theatre was the most appalling thing of its kind we have ever witnessed. They knocked each other down, and trampled on each other, and pushed each other downstairs. They crushed each other up against doors, and kicked each other.[13]

Madge Kendal was also responsible for the production in 1888 of a proto-New Woman adaptation for the stage of another successful woman's novel, *Little Lord Fauntleroy*, by Frances Hodgson Burnett, which, adapted by Burnett herself, became *The Real Little Lord Fauntleroy*, in opposition to the plagiarized version produced by E. V. Seebohm. The Kendal–Burnett version retained the novel's insistence on the power of the bond between mother and son to reform a patriarchal aristocratic system. The audience at the play was dominated by women, at a time when it was not customary for women to go to the theatre unaccom-

76

panied by a man. As a reviewer of the time said: 'It was impossible, if you had the misfortune to be of the sex to which my colleague and I belong, not to feel out of place in a gathering so largely and so impressively female.'[14]

Women's growing presence in the theatrical world as writers, managers and audience was part of a general renewal in the theatre in the last decades of the century, prompted by Ibsen's plays and often associated with Fabian Socialism. The New Drama, in Jill Davies's words, was not simply 'an avant-garde theatre for middle-class intellectuals [but] one of the fields in which emergent social ideas were being explored in representation'.[15] Naturally one of these ideas was 'the woman question'. Fabian Socialism, with its emphasis on the gradual improvement of society, inevitably was influenced by Darwinist thinking and its corollary in eugenicist ideas. Women were vitally important in this respect, not only as the bearers of the next generation but as instrumental in healthy sexual selection. Eugenicist ideas fed on fears about the decline in the birth rate in the late nineteenth century and the unequal breeding capacity of the 'unfit'. As discussed in Chapter 2, this was the degeneration that Max Nordau warned against, and it provides the context to one of the most controversial of New Woman plays, *Alan's Wife*.

Alan's Wife by Florence Bell and Elizabeth Robins (though initially it was staged anonymously, to disguise its authorship from Beerbohm Tree, who was of the opinion that 'women can't write'), first performed at the Independent Theatre in 1893, was a particularly courageous and controversial play. If the stage was becoming more hospitable to women dramatists, for women to write about women's issues brought them an additional challenge, as both actresses and playwrights, adding to an already 'problematic' profession a further dimension of notoriety. Perhaps because of its early date, the fact that it was written, if not produced, by women and because of its shocking subject matter, it may be considered as the first New Woman play by women, though, like much New Woman writing, it is an ambivalent advocate of a feminist cause. Robins's similarly shocking play from around the same time, *The Mirkwater*, did not find a producer; its depiction of a woman who assists her sister's suicide to relieve her from the cancer she suffers from, proving too unpalatable for the London stage.

Alan's Wife is a short play, with a highly focussed plot line, concerning Jean Creyke (played by Elizabeth Robins) whose husband, Alan, 'the handsomest and strongest' of men, 'a man who is my master', is killed in a factory accident. Jean has been a most devoted and dutiful wife and is completely cast down in her widowhood, particularly when the child she gives birth to after Alan's death is born crippled and deformed. After much anguish, during which she baptizes the child herself, she smothers it, believing she relieves it of future suffering. There is a strong suggestion that she also cannot bear that Alan's child should be such an inferior specimen, when its father was so magnificent. In the last act she is condemned to death but is unrepentant. Her courage and integrity as she faces death endow her with heroic status, and in this respect the play registers changing cultural perceptions of infanticide.

As Jo McDonagh has argued,[16] child murder was an important and controversial topic for New Women, 'who in many cases saw themselves as agents of eugenic progress ... highlight[ing] the peculiar contradictions implicit in the discourses on degeneracy. For while the New Women often pictured themselves as warriors against degenerative decline, others perceived them to be symptoms of that very decline.' The play was seen as degenerate, virulently attacked as 'hopeless, heartless, odious'[17] and, in the *Athenaeum's* words, 'shudderingly nude, and its truth of detail ... revolting', with Jean Creyke condemned as a monster. For modern critics,

> there are problems with the play, such as Jean's delighting in Alan's being her 'master', and the suggestion that she kills the child out of some eugenicist notion that he is too imperfect to live. But her decision to smother the baby comes out of love for him and her recognition that she will be unable always to protect and provide for him ... Jean's killing of her child, and silently accepting her death sentence in punishment, are an indictment of an uncaring society. Jean accepts her responsibility and takes control in the only way she sees possible.[18]

The ghost of a child, albeit an aborted child, haunts the most famous play of this time, Elizabeth Robins's *Votes for Women!* Robins was the actress and playwright most closely identified with the feminist movement and it was she who led the way for women to write with confidence about political, social and sexual matters from a woman's perspective. American born, she had arrived in England in 1888 and worked her way through lowly tasks in the theatre before quite rapidly becoming involved in the acting and production of 'advanced' and experimental drama, particularly Ibsen's. Shaw was quite right in seeing plays and productions by women as being more adventurous and experimental than those by men. *Votes for Women!*, first performed at the Royal Court Theatre in April 1907, was a milestone in New Woman drama in both form and content. Originally called 'The Friend of Women', it was re-titled under Harley Granville Barker's direction and was both controversial and highly successful. In the same year as the play was staged, she wrote a version of it as a novel, *The Convert*, the title drawn from her own experience of a suffrage rally in 1906 when she 'first heard women talking politics in public ... and a new chapter was begun for me in the lesson of faith in the capacities of women.'[19]

The play begins like a drawing-room comedy with an assorted cast of aristocrats, marriageable young people and a central love affair, in this case between the young and rather naive Jean Dunbarton, and Geoffrey Stoner, a rising Tory politician. Into this comes Vida Levering, a woman with a past who is now actively involved in building a shelter for destitute women. She and Stoner have obviously known each other before, and this secret relationship provides much of the suspense of the play. In this first Act there is general discussion about the suffragettes. Vida is elegant and beautiful, and thus pointedly contradicts a stereotype of the New Woman and the suffragist: 'it's an exploded notion that the Suffrage women are all dowdy and dull.'

Jean begins to be interested in the suffrage campaign and arranges to attend a meeting that afternoon in London. The second act is a public meeting with various speakers as well as a noisy and challenging crowd. This is a daring innovation, and the means by which Vida and others can express feminist views concerning the double standard, the bias in the justice system, the need for women to have properly paid work, and to be rescued from destitution if they have 'fallen'. Jean is caught up in the cause and realizes that Stoner has something to hide in his relation to Vida.

Act Three is once again a drawing-room setting, this time in Jean's home, with her pressurizing Stoner to make amends for his desertion of Vida long ago. Stoner and Vida talk together about why he could not marry her (because of his father), the child who was aborted, and his regrets. There is also her recognition that marriage and motherhood are not for her but she must use her insight and emotion to further the cause of women's suffrage and also on behalf of women generally. In return for her not exacting vengeance, Stoner agrees to take the cause of reform of the franchise further, partly out of a gratitude that his marriage to Jean can go forward and partly because he now appears to be convinced of the justice of the cause Vida and, by now, Jean are fighting for.

The play is subtitled 'A Dramatic Tract in Three Acts' and the central act is a platform for suffrage propaganda but it is so skilfully done that, well staged, it can have considerable dramatic power, even today. Help with it had come from Granville Barker, who wrote some of the patter for the crowd scene. There are Ibsenite echoes, in that the private story is used, as in *Ghosts*, to illustrate a political/moral theme, and it also aligns with some of Shaw's Fabianite plays such as *Mrs Warren's Profession* or *Widowers' Houses* in its pursuit of a social issue. It was a very topical play, performed at a time in the suffrage movement that Ray Strachey describes as the 'great days', the period between 1906 and 1911, 'when organised societies were expanding [and] when agitation was becoming an exact science'.[20] The year 1907 saw the 'Mud March' when 3,000 bedraggled women walked in pouring rain from Hyde Park Corner to Exeter Hall bearing suffrage banners, with bands playing, including one playing Ethel Smyth's rousing march, 'Votes for Women'. The play alludes to actual events the audience would recognize, such as the mention in Act One of a disturbance in Parliament by women demanding the vote, which occurred on 26 April 1906. Vida Levering's accounts of dying and exploited women was based on an actual account, 'Three Nights in Women's Lodging Houses', by Mary Higgs who had gone into the underworld herself. Ernestine Blunt, the impassioned orator of Act Two, was based, as everyone would recognize, on Christabel Pankhurst.

The play did much to break down 'spheres' in the theatre, showing the way for women to play active political roles in public arenas. Vida Levering reverses the melancholy trend of previous New Women, particularly those who have broken conventional mores, in that she does not have to suffer for her past nor is she trapped in her 'vices' as Shaw's Mrs Warren is. She is also not redeemed by maternity but welcomes life as a single, pioneering woman. The stereotypical comments of Vida's opponents highlight their stale thinking. The character of Vida is an attempt to redefine 'woman' and 'womanliness' in opposition to the stage presences that dominated the theatre of the time. But the play's most important contribution to the debate is its recognition of the links between women's political, sexual and economic dependency. In this respect it is groundbreaking in that it raises the question of abortion without sensationalizing it. The personal is, or becomes, the political, a connection even Stoner has to acknowledge in that what he has done in his private life has repercussions in the public sphere. It is a pleasing addition to the play's success that Robins gave a percentage of her receipts from the play to the Suffrage Society and the Women's Social and Political Union. The following year she was also involved in the formation of the Actresses' Franchise League, one of the many associations created around this time to press for the franchise. The League produced many plays, usually for production at rallies and meetings; they were, as Viv Gardner says, 'unashamedly propagandist'.[21] In an era when to get the message across was of the greatest importance, *Votes for Women!* stands out as fine polemic and also of enduring dramatic interest, with Robins herself as important a feminist figure as the more celebrated Pankhursts.

If maternity is a burden to be shed in *Alan's Wife* and *Votes for Women!*, a more positive account of a woman's relationship with her child comes in *Rutherford and Son* by Githa Sowerby, first produced at the Court Theatre in 1912. Like *The Last of the Mullins*, it shows the decline of patriarchal authority, the general dependency of women and, running counter to this, the power of maternal love in making a woman strong. It also shows men's weakness and dependency, especially when they have been bullied by a tyrannical father figure. The story concerns the firm of Rutherford, dominated by John Rutherford, a hard-working, successful engineering works owner, a self-made man whose snobbishness includes keeping his daughter, Janet, in imprisoned idleness. In his household there is also his sister Ann, a querulous, ageing spinster, and his son John, daughter-in-law Mary and their baby, and his other son Richard, who is a weak and ineffectual clergyman. There is also Martin, a works foreman, who, it emerges, is having a secret affair with Janet. The play conveys very vividly the family's discontents and joylessness, and how it gradually falls apart, with son John leaving after finding his father has bullied Martin into giving him the receipt for a new invention, Janet turned out of doors because of her affair, and Richard accepting a curacy a long way away. Loyalty to the Rutherford firm has prompted Martin to betray John's secret but in spite of this he is dismissed. Janet urges him to start a new life with her but he is a broken man, unable to give love to Janet because of his commitment to Rutherford's. Up to this point the play has seemed to have hardly any feminist message but at the end, with only John's wife Mary remaining, does this 'weak' and overlooked woman assert her authority. She bargains with Rutherford over her son, ensuring that he and she will be kept and the boy educated until he is 10, when she will allow Rutherford to have charge of him. She knows that by then Rutherford will be an old man, unable to do much damage to his grandson.

Throughout the play there has been an emphasis on the firm of Rutherford's being passed from father to son, and the old man knows that this is his only chance to secure an heir. Though Mary is mild, not well educated or middle class, and now abandoned by her husband, her love for her son emboldens her to bargain with and indeed to triumph over the old man. Less emancipated than Janet in *The Last of the De Mullins* in that she remains trapped in the patriarchal home, Mary's fate is somehow more credible than Janet's hat-shop escape, which by comparison seems implausible.

The play is an example of the new realism of the Edwardian Theatre, which encouraged an emphasis on the economic realities of life and the dull routine of most people's lives, particularly women trapped at home. Women's dependency is prominent in *Votes for Women!* and *Rutherford and Son* but their circumstances are comfortably affluent. In *Diana of Dobson's* by Cecily Hamilton and even more in Elizabeth Baker's *Chains*, it is the lower middle class who feature, clerks and shop-girls, respect-able but penurious, working long hours in monotonous jobs, often under despotic managers or owners. The portrayal of mean, struggling lives is reminiscent of novels of the period, Arnold Bennett's *The Old Wives' Tale*, *Clayhanger* and *Hilda Lessways*, for example, all published between 1908 and 1911. These novels also have if not exactly New Women, then independent and aspiring women who look for, even if they do not find, fortunes beyond the common lot of women. The classic novel in respect of the Edwardian New Woman was H. G. Wells's *Ann Veronica* (1908) and for the downtrodden shop worker, *The History of Mr Polly* (1910).

Diana of Dobson's, which was first performed at the Kingsway Theatre in 1908, opens in a dormitory for assistants in a draper's shop, all complaining of the constrained and miserable life they lead. Diana Massingberd is the most vocal in her complaints and is frequently in trouble for insubordination. She receives a letter telling her that she has inherited £300, and she determines to have one glorious month spending it. The second Act sees her spending it in a smart hotel in Switzerland where she has transformed herself into the well-dressed Mrs Massingberd, reputedly a wealthy widow. She is courted by a rich, elderly manufacturer and by a rather feckless young man, Bretherton, whose £600 a year does not keep him in the style he wishes. When he asks Diana to marry him, she tells him the truth, and when he objects to her behaviour she points out that it is no different from his. She refuses the rich older man; however desperate her life at Dobson's she does not wish to sell herself into a life of married imprisonment with a man she does not love. The final Act is a romantic reconciliation between Diana and Bretherton on the Thames Embankment where he is sleeping rough in an attempt to prove that he can earn his own living and not be the spineless man she has taken him for. She too is impecunious, being unable to find work and all her inheritance gone. They decide to get married and make the best of his £600 a year.

The play is an uneasy mixture of realistic descriptions of the life of shop girls, drawing-room comedy – the hotel in Switzer-land – and sentimentality on the moonlit Embankment. This last is at first sight surprising since Cicely Hamilton, an active suffragist and writer of suffrage plays, was probably best known for her tract *Marriage as a Trade* (1909) in which she shows how young women are groomed to be bought into marriage as the only career open to them. However, the play is less of a capitulation than it might at first seem. Diana is well aware of this economic compulsion to avoid the 'grind and squalor and tyranny and overwork' of a place like Dobson's drapery emporium. As she says to the younger Kitty in Act One, 'In three months you'll be married. However your marriage turns out, it will be a change for you – a change from the hosiery department of Dobson's.' Yet she does not take a way out of Dobson's by marrying her wealthy suitor. In the hard-hitting dialogue in Act Three, when she and Bretherton each confess their poverty, she makes clear to him the exploitative and mercenary nature of marriage; 'I am an adventuress, Captain Bretherton, what are you but an adventurer?' But a marriage for love rather than money is, apparently, an acceptable union.

More credible and even-toned is *Chains* by Elizabeth Baker, which was first performed by the Play Actors at the Court Theatre in 1909, with moderate success. Its reception was patronizing, assuming that its realism was simply transcribed autobiography and that its low-key style and narrow frame of reference were due to ignorance on the part of the dramatist. The *Era* said that the piece 'might be made suitable for production in a West End theatre if it received certain strengthening touches at the hands of an experienced dramatist'. As Linda Fitzsimmons notes,[22] Baker 'presents the notion that marriage is a woman's only possible course of action in a highly critical manner' and does so through the astute use of theatrical devices, such as the off-stage action that the audience can see, the secret the audience knows but not the characters, and the careful orchestration of their exits and entrances. In spite of the contemporary assumption that Elizabeth Baker was a one-off playwright, she wrote some fifteen plays, her last being produced in 1931. Her protagonists are invariably working women: milliners, dressmakers, secretaries, domestic servants.

The setting for *Chains* is lower middle-class, and takes place either in the sitting-room in Lily and Charley's house, or that of Lily's parents. It is the world of respectable clerks and typists, or shop assistants, with Lily and Charley having to take in lodgers

to make ends meet. One of their lodgers announces that he is
going to emigrate to Australia. This makes Charley restless and
to the very last minutes of the play he plans to accompany the
lodger, unbeknown to Lily, leaving her behind. But her an-
nouncement that she is pregnant defeats his plans and he is
resigned to stay, to continue working at the safe but boring job
he hates. These are the chains of marriage, as much chains as the
routines of the work he does as a clerk or the stiff collar he is
forced to wear.

This hardly seems to be a New Woman play, except that
Charley's sister-in-law, Maggie, stakes her claim to a kind of
independence that is peculiar to women. She is engaged to a
comfortably-off but boring man who adores her, but whom she
does not love, and she breaks off the engagement. Marriage to
him would free her from the shop work she hates but she will
not exchange the chains of work, which she can break at any
time if she wishes, for the chains of marriage, which, particularly
as it would be to a man who would not be unkind to her, she
could never break. In the final act, Act Four, she says: 'I don't
love Walter, only his house. Now, I can leave the shop any day,
when I've saved enough – and run away. But I couldn't run
away from Walter.' Maggie also blames women like Lily for
holding men back: 'It's the women who make men afraid . . .
they say to the men: – "I shouldn't trouble, my dear, if I were
you. You're safe here. Do be careful."' This has been Lily's
theme all along, refusing to entertain Charley's ideas of emigra-
ting and stressing how safe his job is. At the end of the play,
when Maggie hears of Lily's pregnancy, and that Charley now
knows about it, she says to Lily, 'So you've *got* him after all.' The
play ends with Charley struggling to put on his 'beastly collar'.

Chains is a play that deserved to be shown more respect than
the London critics gave it, and it is fitting that it had considerable
success in provincial repertory. The Gaiety Theatre in Manchester, for example, managed and sponsored by Annie Horniman
from 1907 when she left the Abbey Theatre in Dublin, produced
the play in 1911. As Elaine Aston points out, under Horniman's
direction, the Gaiety's dramatic output, though it 'included
foreign plays in translation, revivals of classic pieces and
contemporary lyrical drama',[23] in its New Drama was heavily
weighted towards 'the Woman Question'. Its most famous

production was of *Hindle Wakes* by Stanley Houghton, in 1913, in which a young woman refuses to marry the man she has slept with, to the great disquiet of her parents. As Aston says, the play argues 'for a women's right to sexual pleasure outside marriage'.

By this time, the era of New Drama, and New Woman drama, is drawing to a close. The Great War looms, and when it is over in 1918 there is a new world of partial female suffrage, an excess of women over men of one and a half million, and a new kind of feminism, of a kind in which social responsibility will be the dominant note. Elizabeth Robins will be there too, adapting to the new conditions as a member of the Six Point Group and a founding contributor to the feminist journal *Time and Tide*.

Notes

CHAPTER 1. AN INTRODUCTION TO THE NEW WOMAN

1. Marie Corelli, *The Sorrows of Satan* (1895) Peter Keating (ed.) (Oxford: Oxford University Press, 1998), 7, 178.
2. Ibid. 308–9.
3. Lisa Tickner, *The Spectacle of Women: Images of the Suffrage Campaign, 1907–1914* (London: Chatto & Windus, 1987), 183.
4. Constance Rover, *Love, Morals and the Feminists* (London: Routledge & Kegan Paul, 1970), 132.
5. Ann Heilmann, *New Women Fiction: Women Writing First Wave Feminism* (Basingstoke: Macmillan, 2000), 22. See also Michelle Elizabeth Tusan, 'Inventing the New Woman: Print Culture and Identity Politics During the Fin-de-Siècle', *Victorian Periodicals Review* 31.2 (Summer 1998), 169–82.
6. Grand's article appeared in the *North American Review* 158 (March 1894), and Ouida's reply appeared in the May issue of the same journal. Both novelists wrote under pseudonyms; Grand was Frances Elizabeth McFall and Ouida was Marie Louise de Ramée.
7. Quoted Ellen Jordan, 'The Christening of the New Woman: May 1894', *Victorian Newsletter* (Spring 1983), 20.
8. Ibid. 19–21.
9. David Rubinstein, *Before the Suffragettes: Women's Emancipation in the 1890s* (Brighton: Harvester, 1986), 16.
10. The Langham Place group, for example, so called because they met at the home of Barbara Leigh Smith, campaigned from the 1850s for the suffrage and also for improved working conditions and educational opportunities for women, and the rights of married women. Members included Emily Davies, Lydia Becker, Mrs Jacob Bright, Barbara Leigh Smith (later Bodichon), Frances Power Cobbe and Bessie Rayner Parkes.

11. This was followed in 1882 by a second Married Women's Property Act which allowed a woman to keep inherited and other non-earned property, and to be responsible for her debts.
12. Ray Strachey, *The Cause* (London: Virago Press, 1978), 275–85. Martha Vicinus *Independent Women: Work and Community for Single Women, 1850–1920* (London: 1985), 247–50, gives 1884 as the year in which women's attempt to get the vote was decisively defeated.
13. H. M. Hyndman, 'English Workers as They Are' (1887), quoted Elaine Showalter, *Sexual Anarchy: Gender and Culture at the Fin de Siècle* (London: Bloomsbury, 1991), 5.
14. The 1851 census was the first attempt to count occupations in any detail.
15. David Rubinstein points out that women were increasingly employed 'less because of the demands of feminists ... than in response to the needs of business, the professions and government for docile, well-educated and cheap labour'. *Before the Suffragettes*, x.
16. See John Burnett (ed.), *Useful Toil: Autobiographies of Working People from the 1820s to the 1920s* (London: Allen Lane, 1974), 135–74.
17. 'Report on the Money Wages of Indoor Domestic Servants' (Vol. 42, Parliamentary Papers, 1899), 111, quoted Burnett (ed.), *Useful Toil*, 161.
18. Other manual workers at this time earned considerably more: for example, a male spinner could earn 40/- a week and a female 23/- a week. But agricultural workers probably had the lowest pay of any group of workers, with wages as low as 6/- a week in some parts of the country. See Burnett, *Useful Toil*, 24–54.
19. Rubinstein, *Before the Suffragettes*, xiii.
20. Beatrice Webb, *My Apprenticeship* (1926) (Harmondsworth: Penguin, 1971), 264.
21. *The Diaries of Beatrice Webb*, ed. Norman and Jeanne MacKenzie (London: Virago, 2000), 48, 75.
22. Sally Ledger, *The New Woman: Fiction and Feminism at the Fin de Siècle* (Manchester: Manchester University Press, 1997), 16.
23. See David Rubinstein, 'Cycling in the 1890s', *Victorian Studies* 21 (1977), 47–71.
24. This was the winning verse from a competition in *Woman* magazine (Sept. 1894), quoted Gail Cunningham, *The New Woman and the Victorian Novel* (London: Macmillan, 1978), 1.
25. See Lynn Pykett, *The Improper Feminine: The Women's Sensation Novel and the New Woman Writing* (London: Routledge, 1992), 139, 150.
26. Hope Malleson, *A Woman Doctor: Mary Murdoch of Hull* (London: Sidgwick and Jackson, 1919), 65.

27. Holbrook Jackson, *The Eighteen Nineties: A Review of Art and Ideas at the close of the Nineteenth Century* (Brighton: Harvester Press, 1976), 21–2.
28. Showalter, *Sexual Anarchy*, 2–3.
29. Ralph Iron, pseud. Olive Schreiner, *The Story of An African Farm* (London: Chapman & Hall, 1883).
30. Florence Nightingale, 'Cassandra', in Strachey, *The Cause*, 396, 413.
31. S. Ledger and R. Luckhurst (eds.), *The Fin de Siècle: A Reader in Cultural History c. 1880–1900* (Oxford: Oxford University Press, 2000), 94–5.
32. Ibid. 95.
33. Ledger, *The New Woman*, 124.
34. Rover, *Love, Morals and the Feminists*, 2.
35. *Contemporary Review*, 67 (1895), 630.
36. Quoted Ledger, *The New Woman*, 188.
37. Ledger and Luckhurst, *The Fin de Siècle*, 79.
38. Judith R. Walkowitz, *City of Dreadful Delight: Narratives of Sexual Danger in Late-Victorian London* (London: Virago Press, 1992), 81–168.
39. Ledger and Luckhurst, *The Fin de Siècle*, 333.
40. Angelique Richardson, *Love and Eugenics in the Late Nineteenth Century: Rational Reproduction and the New Woman* (Oxford: Oxford University Press, 2003), 3.
41. Ibid. 27.
42. Ibid. 173.
43. Richardson, *Love and Eugenics in the Late Nineteenth Century*, 192.
44. Ledger and Luckhurst, *The Fin de Siècle*, 328.
45. C. F. G. Masterman, *From the Abyss* (1902) (New York, Garland, n.d.), 2.
46. Gerd Bjørhovde, *Rebellious Structures: Women Writers and the Crisis of the Novel 1880–1900* (Oslo: Norwegian University Press, 1987), 79.
47. Ann Heilmann, *New Woman Fiction*, 98.
48. Eleanor Marx and Edward Aveling, 'The Woman Question, from a Socialist Point of View', *Westminster Review*, 6.25 (1885), 214.
49. Ledger, *The New Woman*, 94.
50. Quoted Kate Flint, *The Woman Reader 1837–1914* (Oxford: Clarendon Press, 1993), 311.
51. Flint, *The Woman Reader*, 305.
52. Hugh Stutfield, 'The Psychology of Feminism', *Blackwood's Magazine*, 161 (1897), 115.
53. Elizabeth Robins, 'The Women Writers', *Way Stations* (1913), 5.
54. Quoted Ledger, *The New Woman*, 188.

55. George Egerton, 'A Cross Line', originally published in *Keynotes* (1893), reproduced in Elaine Showalter (ed.), *Daughters of Decadence: Women Writers of the Fin-de-Siècle* (London: Virago Press, 1993), 47–68.
56. Flint, *The Woman Reader*, 294–6.

CHAPTER 2. GENDER, LITERARY VALUE AND THE WOMAN OF GENIUS

1. Angelique Richardson has discussed how New Woman writers deplored the unacceptability of such themes in 'unhealthy' male-authored romances. For a perceptive discussion of Sarah Grand's and Mona Caird's relative positions on thematics of health and the role of fiction see Richardson, 'Allopathic Pills? Health, Fitness and New Woman Fictions', *Woman: A Cultural Review* (Spring, 1999), 1–21.
2. Ann Heilmann, *New Woman Fiction: Women Writing First Wave Feminism* (London: Macmillan, 2000), 9. See also Jane Eldridge Miller, *Rebel Women: Modernism, Feminism and the Edwardian Novel* (London: Virago, 1994), 18.
3. Rita S. Kranidis, *Subversive Discourse* (Basingstoke: Macmillan, 1995).
4. Andreas Huyssen, *After the Great Divide: Modernism, Mass Culture and Postmodernism* (London: Macmillan, 1986), 47.
5. See ibid. and Rita Felski, *The Gender of Modernity* (London: Harvard University Press, 1995).
6. Edmund Gosse, 'The Decay of Literary Taste', *North American Review* 161 (1895), 109–18.
7. Ibid. 112.
8. Ibid. 117.
9. Ibid. 115.
10. Hardy wrote of New Woman novels to Edward Clodd that, ' "[o]wing, I suppose to the accident of its appearance just after the sheaf of purpose-novels we have had lately on the marriage question, – though written long before them – some of the papers class mine with them – though the case of my people is one of temperamental unfitness for the contract, peculiar to the family of the parties" ' (10 Nov. 1895). Letter from T. Hardy to E. Clodd, Clodd Archive, Brotherton Library, University of Leeds.
11. It ran to nineteen editions in its first year of publication. See Juliet Gardiner, *The New Woman* (London: Collins and Brown, 1993), 171.
12. Grant Allen, *The British Barbarians* (1895) (London: Garland Publishing, 1977).

13. George Moore, 'Literature at Nurse, or, Circulating Morals' (London: Vizetelly, 1885) rpt. (Sussex: Harvester Press, 1976).
14. E. L. Linton, 'Candour in English Fiction', *New Review* (Jan.1890), 6–21 (10).
15. Ethelmer was the pseudonym of Elizabeth Wolstenholme and her common-law husband, Ben Elmy. For detail of Wolstenholme's career and relationship with Elmy and the woman's movement, see Sandra Stanley Holton, 'Free Love and Victorian Feminism: The Divers Matrimonials of Elizabeth Wolstenholme and Ben Elmy', *Victorian Studies* 37:2 (Winter, 1994), 199–222.
16. *Womanhood* (1899–1907) was 'an illustrated magazine of literature, art, science, medicine and hygiene and the progress of women'.
17. 'The Tree of Knowledge', *New Review* 10:61 (June 1894), 675–90. Participants: Madame Adam, the Rev. H. Adler, Chief Rabbi, Walter Besant, Bjørnsjerne Bjørnsen, Hall Caine, Madame Sarah Grand, Mrs Edmund Gosse, Thomas Hardy, Mrs Lynn Linton, Max Nordau, Lady Henry Somerset, Baroness Von Suttner, Miss Frances E. Willard and Israel Zangwill.
18. For discussion of the series in relation to contemporary positions on sex education, see Claudia Nelson, ' "Under the guidance of a Wise Mother": British Sex Education at the Fin de Siècle' in Claudia and Ann Sumner Homes (eds.), *Maternal Instincts: Visions of Motherhood and Sexuality in Britain: 1875–1925* (London: Macmillan, 1997), 103–4.
19. 'Aurora', 'Between the Lights', *Signal* (June 1894), 412.
20. Lady Susan Mary Elizabeth Jeune, 'The Revolt of the Daughters', *Fortnightly Review* 55 (1 March 1894), 267–76.
21. B. A. Crackanthorpe, 'The Revolt of the Daughters', *Nineteenth Century* 35 (1894), 23 LVMQ, II.
22. Ibid. 269.
23. William Barry in the *Quarterly Review* vol. 179 no. 358 (1894), 289–318 (295).
24. *Signal* 2:36 (6 Sept.1894), 146.
25. See Elaine Showalter, *The Female Malady: Women, Madness and English Culture 1830–1980* (London: Virago, 1987).
26. Linton, 'Candour in English Fiction', 6–21 (11).
27. Ibid. 14.
28. Ibid.
29. The leading French Naturalist writer Emile Zola (1840–1902) aimed at realism based on a thorough medical precision and the 'rigour of scientific truth'; Emile Zola, 'Le Roman Expérimental', *Le Roman Expérimental* (1880) included in *Documents of Literary Realism*, George J. Becker (ed.) (Princeton: Princeton University Press, 1973),

162–96. Zola's methodology was grounded in the work of Dr Claude Bernard in his *Introduction to the Study of Experimental Medicine* (1865). Zola claimed that the intercourse between the fields of medicine and literature could bring to light the 'truth' of human behaviours and their grounding in the discoveries of evolutionary science.

30. Teresa Mangum, *Married, Middlebrow, and Militant: Sarah Grand and the New Woman Novel* (Ann Arbor: University of Michigan Press, 1998), 178.

31. Richardson, 'Allopathic Pills? Health, Fitness and New Woman Fictions', 15.

32. Alison in *The Story of a Modern Woman* describes the metropolitan pleasures she had enjoyed in Paris of riding freely on the tops of omnibuses, and the 'charming' trams (*SMW* 48); Mary Erle walks to the British Library, and in *The Beth Book*, Beth finds 'in the new view of London and of London life from the top of omnibuses more of the unexpected, of delight, of beauty for the eyes and of matter for the mind' (*BB* 495). Amy Levy's poem, 'Ballade of an Omnibus' (1888) records such rides with humour.

33. Deborah L. Parsons, *Streetwalking the Metropolis: Women, the City and Modernity* (Oxford University Press, 2000), 7.

34. Ibid. 41.

35. For example, East End charity workers, the Salvation Army's 'Sisters of Mercy' feature in Margaret Harkness's novel *In Darkest London* (1891), and in Caird's *The Daughters of Danaus*, Hadria's younger sister Algitha undertakes philanthropic work in the East End. For further discussion see Sally Ledger, *The New Woman: Fiction and Feminism at the Fin de Siècle* (Manchester: Manchester University Press, 1997), 154.

36. Ledger, *The New Woman*, 159.

37. Heilmann, *New Woman Fiction*, 184.

38. The opening remarks by Francis Galton in the 1892 edition of *Hereditary Genius: An Inquiry into its Laws and Consequences* (1869) suggest the degree to which opinions conflicted on the nature of 'genius'. He regretted that he had not entitled his book 'Hereditary Ability', because he wanted to communicate that the specific quality of genius was innate: ' "*Hereditary Genius* therefore seemed to be a more expressive and just title than *Hereditary Ability*, for ability does not exclude the effects of education, which genius does." ' Francis Galton, *Hereditary Genius: An Enquiry into Its Laws and Consequences* (1869) (reprint second ed. 1892; Gloucester, Mass.: Peter Smith, 1972), 26.

39. Penny Boumelha, 'The Woman of Genius and the Woman of Grub Street', *English Literature in Transition* 40:2 (1997), 164–81 (172).

40. Vernon Lee, *Limbo and other Essays* (London: Grant Richards, 1897), 2.
41. Heilmann, *New Woman Fiction*, 165.
42. Margaret Morganroth Gullette (ed.), Afterword, *The Daughters of Danaus*, 513.
43. We find a similar feminine lack of desire for literary success professed by the best-selling author, Marie Corelli, in her autobiographical account of her first book: 'I had no sort of literary pride in my work whatsoever; there was nothing of self in the wish I had, that my ideas, such as they were, should reach the public, for I had no particular need of money, and certainly no hankering after fame', Marie Corelli in Jerome K. Jerome (eds.), *My First Book: The Experiences of Walter Besant et al.* (London: Chatto and Windus, 1894), 207.
44. This short story was first published in a collection: Sarah Grand, *Emotional Moments* (London: Hurst and Blackett, 1908), 303–58.
45. Heilmann suggests that 'The Undefinable' is about a woman artist 'subverting the stereotypical role of the muse, Grand's female artist poses as a model'. She argues that '[i]t is the woman artist who is infused with "genius".' Heilmann, *New Woman Fiction*, 160.

CHAPTER 3. NEW WOMAN WRITERS' WORKS

1. For details see Lucy Bland, *Banishing the Beast: English Feminism and Sexual Morality 1885 –1914* (Harmondsworth: Penguin, 1995).
2. August Weismann, *Essays upon Heredity and Kindred Biological Problems*, Edward B. Poulton, Selmar Schönland and Arthur E. Shipley (eds.) (Oxford: Clarendon, 1889).
3. Elaine Showalter, 'Syphilis, Sexuality, and the Fiction of the *Fin de Siècle*' in Lyn Pykett (ed.), *Reading Fin de Siècle Fictions* (London: Longman, 1996), 167.
4. For a discussion of Sarah Grand's and Mona Caird's relative positions on thematics of health and the role of fiction see Angelique Richardson, 'Allopathic Pills? Health, Fitness and New Woman Fictions', *Woman: A Cultural Review* (Spring 1999), 1–21.
5. Sarah A. Tooley, 'The Woman's Question: An Interview with Madame Sarah Grand', *Humanitarian*, vol. 8 (1896), 169.
6. *Shafts* 2:5 (July 1893), 92.
7. See for example, *Athenaeum* 34.12 (18 March 1893), 342. *Lippincott's Magazine* 52 (1893), 637–40.
8. Grand's direct endorsement of the eugenics of Galton is evident in Evadne's anti-Catholic lament on the Church before the reformation: ' "the Church, with that curious want of foresight for which it is peculiar, induced the saints to put themselves away in barren

celibacy so that their saintliness could not spread while it encouraged sinners saturated with vice to transmit their misery making propensities from generation to generation." ' (*THT* 340). This passage paraphrases Galton in *Hereditary Genius*. In the chapter, 'Influences that affect the natural ability of nations' Galton vented his spleen on the Church for its history of un-eugenic policies concerning the monks and nuns: 'the Church chose to preach and exact celibacy. The consequence was that these gentle natures had no continuance, and thus by a policy so singularly unwise and suicidal . . . the Church brutalised the breed of our forefathers." ' Francis Galton, *Hereditary Genius* (1869; 2nd edn. 1892) (Gloucester, Mass.: Peter Smith, 1972), 411.

9. Unsigned review; probably editor Margaret Shurmer Sibthorp, *Shafts* (Feb.1897), 47.

10. Emma Frances Brooke, *The Superfluous Woman* (London: William Heinemann, 1894).

11. *The Woman's Signal* (14 March 1894).

12. For an insightful discussion of this novel see Sally Ledger, *The New Woman: Fiction and Feminism at the Fin de Siècle* (Manchester: Manchester University Press, 1997).

13. Ann Heilmann, *New Woman Fiction: Women Writing First Wave Feminism* (London: Macmillan, 2000), 89.

14. ' "More mournfully tragical than these mysterious personal chains are the inherited tendencies with which we are born, the preformed habit which is in us at our birth. Who has striven against some evil inheritance, that has lifted himself out of it by main force of will, does not know the rapture of a relapsed moment? Nature mocks us with this trick of reversion. Behind the mounting steps of Evolution creeps the stealthy shadow of Atavism, like old guilt which can never be repudiated any more." ' (*SW* 118)

15. Charles Darwin, *The Expression of the Emotions in Man and Animals* (1872).

16. See Margaret Morganroth Gullette, Afterword, *The Daughters of Danaus* (New York: The Feminist Press 1989), 493–534.

17. Heilmann, *New Woman Fiction* and Angelique Richardson (ed.), *Women Who Did; Stories by Men and Women, 1890–1914* (London: Penguin, 2002) have critically differentiated Caird's critiques of motherhood from her peers.

18. Lyn Pykett 'The Cause of Women and the Course of Fiction: The Case of Mona Caird' in Christopher Parker (ed.), *Gender Roles and Sexuality in Victorian Literature* (Aldershot: Scolar Press, 1995), 125–38 (132).

19. Lyn Pykett calls Caird's *Pathway of the Gods* (1898) which deals with legends, a 'strange and mystical novel', whose *fin-de-siècle* mysticism is emblematic of its use of modernist techniques. Ibid, 135.

20. Matthew Arnold wrote at length about the contribution of Celtic writers to English literature in his Oxford lectures printed in the *Cornhill* (1866) and in *On the Study of Celtic Literature* (London: Smith, Elder and Co., 1867) which continued to be widely read later in the century.

21. See Havelock Ellis, 'The Ancestry of Genius', *Atlantic Monthly* (March 1893), 383–9.

22. For contemporary theory on the reversion to ancestral states and relationship to the will, see Henry Maudsley, *Body and Will: Being An Essay Concerning Will In Its Metaphysical, Physiological and Pathological Aspects* (London: Kegan Paul, Trench & Co., 1883), 26.

23. For discussion of the relationship of the New Woman to imperialism, see Ch. 3 of Sally Ledger's *The New Woman*. Angelique Richardson examines the relationship of the New Woman to eugenics in depth in *The Eugenisation of Love: Darwin, Galton and Late Nineteenth-Century Fictions of Heredity and Eugenics* (Oxford: Oxford University Press, 2003).

24. Carol. L. Barash, 'Virile Womanhood: Olive Schreiner's Narratives of a Master Race' in Elaine Showalter (ed.), *Speaking of Gender* (London: Routledge, 1989), 270.

25. Ledger, *The New Woman*, 86.

26. Karl Pearson, 'Woman and Labour', *Fortnightly Review* (1888), 561–77 (569).

27. Karl Pearson, 'The Woman's Question', *The Ethic of Freethought* (London: Adam and Charles Black, 1888), 394.

28. Ledger, *The New Woman*, 43.

29. Hugh E. M. Stutfield, 'Tommyrotics', *Blackwood's Edinburgh Magazine* 157 (1895), 833–45. Anon, *Critic* (26 May 1894), 354.

30. For example, John Sutherland (1990), and Carolyn Christensen Nelson, *British Women Fiction Writers of the 1890s* (London: Twaynes, 1996).

31. *Shafts* (8 March 1894), 153–4.

32. Ibid. 153.

33. Ibid. 153.

34. See Melisa Brittain, 'Erasing Race in the New Woman Review: Victoria Cross's *Anna Lombard*', *Nineteenth Century Feminisms* 4 (Spring/Summer 2001), 75–95.

35. Nancy Paxton cites that in '1901 for example, (the British) numbered approximately 170,000 in a total Indian population of 294,000,000 and Eurasian population of 89,000'. Nancy L .Paxton, *Writing Under the Raj: Gender, Race and Rape in the British Colonial Imagination* (London: Rutgers University Press, 1999), 193.

36. For discussion of the *femme fatale* see Rebecca Stott, *The Late-Victorian Femme Fatale: The Kiss of Death* (London: Macmillan, 1992), 30.

37. Shoshana Milgram Knapp, 'Revolutionary Androgyny in the fiction of "Victoria Cross"' in Carola M. Kaplan and Anne B. Simpson (eds.), *Seeing Double: Revisioning Edwardian and Modernist Literature* (St Martin's Press: New York, 1996), 17.

38. Josephine McDonagh, 'Infanticide and the Boundaries of Culture from Hume to Arnold' in Carol Barash and Susan C. Greenfield (eds.), *Inventing Maternity: Politics, Science, and Literature, 1650–1865* (Lexington: University Press of Kentucky, 1999), 225.

39. Ella D'Arcy's stories were published in collections, *Monochromes* (1895) and *Modern Instances* (1898).

40. Milgram Knapp, 'Revolutionary Androgyny in the fiction of "Victoria Cross"', 4.

41. This cross-dressing moment is developed into an adventure for her later novel *Six Chapters of a Man's Life* (1903). For further discussion of this novel see Milgram Knapp, 'Revolutionary Androgyny in the fiction of "Victoria Cross"', 12–14.

42. Borgia Smudgiton (Owen Seaman), 'She Notes', *Punch* (10 and 17 March 1894), 109, 129. Republished in Angelique Richardson (ed.), *Women Who Did*.

43. Hugh Stutfield, 'Tommyrotics', *Blackwood's Magazine*, 157 (June 1895).

44. Sally Ledger (ed.) in Introduction, George Egerton, *Keynotes and Discords* (Birmingham: University of Birmingham Press, 2003).

45. Heilmann, *New Woman Fiction*, 45.

46. Of the 'Woman Question' Lee wrote, 'I must begin by confessing that the question which goes by that name had never attracted my attention, or, rather, that I had on every occasion evaded and avoided it', 'The Economic Parasitism of Women', *North American Review* 175 (July 1902), 71–90.

47. Violet Paget quoted in Peter Gunn, *Vernon Lee: Violet Paget 1856–1935* (London: Oxford University Press, 1964), 106. Also in Burdett Gardner, *The Lesbian Imagination (Victorian Style): A Psychological and Critical Study of 'Vernon Lee'* (New York: Garland, 1987), 376–7.

48. Kathy Alexis Psomiades has suggested that *Miss Brown* is a 'lesbian text' on these grounds. See '"Still Burning from This Strangling Embrace": Vernon Lee on Desire and Aesthetics', in Richard Dellamara (ed.), *Victorian Sexual Dissidence* (London: Chicago University Press, 1999), 21–41 (28).

49. See Hilary Fraser, 'Women and the Ends of Art History, Vision and Corporeality in Nineteenth-Century Critical Discourse'. *Victorian Studies* 42:1 (Autumn 1998/1999), 77–100.

50. The artist's act of expressing his/her internal world was problematized by the decadents: as Arthur Symons, a leading voice in the

English Decadent literary movement, had put it: 'this endeavour after a perfect truth to one's impression, to one's intuition – perhaps an impossible endeavour –'. Arthur Symons, 'The Decadent Movement in Literature', *Harper's New Monthly Magazine* (Nov. 1893) reprinted in *Arthur Symons: Selected Writings*, ed. Roger Holdsworth (Manchester: Carcanet Press, 1989), 74.

51. See Ruth Robbins, 'Apparitions can be deceptive: Vernon Lee's Androgynous Spectres' in Ruth Robbins and Julian Wolfreys (eds.), *Victorian Gothic: Literary and Cultural Manifestations in the Nineteenth Century* (Basingstoke: Palgrave, 2000), 182–200. Angela Leighton, 'Ghosts, Aestheticism, and "Vernon Lee"', *Victorian Literature and Culture* (2000), 1–14.

52. Terry Castle, *The Apparitional Lesbian: Female Homosexuality and Modern Culture* (New York: Columbia University, 1993), 56.

53. In Ovid's *Metamorphoses*, Pygmalion was the king of Cyprus, a sculptor who fell in love with the life-like ivory statue he had created. He prayed to the goddess Aphrodite to give him a wife resembling the feminine ideal, and the goddess brought his statue, Galatea, to life.

54. *The Woman's Signal* (7 June 1894), 312.

CHAPTER 4. NEW WOMAN DRAMA

1. Elizabeth Robins, *Way Stations* (1913), quoted Sheila Stowell, *A Stage of Their Own* (Manchester: Manchester University Press, 1992), 13.

2. *The New Woman and Other Emancipated Woman Plays*, edited and with an introduction by Jean Chothia (Oxford: Oxford University Press, 1998), 17.

3. Sally Ledger, *The New Woman: Fiction and Feminism at the Fin de Siècle* (Manchester: Manchester University Press, 1997), 38.

4. Chothia, *The New Woman*, xix.

5. Ibid. 113.

6. Kerry Powell, *Women and Victorian Theatre* (Cambridge: Cambridge University Press, 1997), 37.

7. Constance Fenimore Woolson, 'Miss Grief' in *Daughters of Decadence*, Elaine Showalter (ed.) (London: Virago, 1993), 165–91.

8. Viv Gardner and Susan Rutherford (eds.), *The New Woman and Her Sisters: Feminism and the Theatre 1850–1914* (Hemel Hempstead: Harvester Wheatsheaf, 1992), Introduction, 1–14 (7).

9. Powell, *Women and Victorian Theatre*, 125.

10. Ibid. 114.

11. Gardner and Rutherford (eds.), *The New Woman and Her Sisters*, 7–8.

12. Powell, *Women and Victorian Theatre*, 167.
13. *Playgoer* (Aug. 1889), quoted Powell, *Women and Victorian Theatre*, 71.
14. *Illustrated Sporting and Dramatic News* (July 1888), quoted Powell, *Women and Victorian Theatre*, 116.
15. Gill Davies, 'The New Woman and the New Life' in Gardner and Rutherford (eds.) *The New Woman and Her Sisters*, 17–36 (18).
16. Josephine McDonagh, *Child Murder and British Culture, 1720–1900* (Cambridge: Cambridge University Press, 2003), 179. An interesting comparison can be made with Victoria Cross's novel *Anna Lombard* (1901) where the baby is murdered because it is a product of 'degenerate' miscegenation.
17. Viv Gardner, 'Women and Writing at the *Fin de siècle*', in Marion Shaw (ed.), *An Introduction to Women's Writing from the Middle Ages to the Present Day* (London: Prentice Hall, 1998), 177–202 (184).
18. Adrienne Scullion (ed.), *Female Playwrights of the Nineteenth Century* (London: Everyman, 1996), 453.
19. Elizabeth Robins, *Way Stations*, quoted in Chothia , *The New Woman*, xxi.
20. Ray Strachey, *The Cause: A Short History of the Women's Movement in Great Britain* (London: Virago, 1978), 305.
21. Gardner, 'Women and Writing at the *Fin de Siècle*', 196.
22. Linda Fitzsimmons, 'New Woman Plays', in Linda Fitzsimmons and Viv Gardner (eds.), *New Woman Plays* (London: Methuen, 1991), 82.
23. Elaine Aston, 'The "New Woman" at Manchester's Gaiety Theatre' in Gardner and Rutherford (eds.), *The New Woman and Her Sisters*, 205–20 (207).

Select Bibliography

WORKS AND EDITIONS OF WORKS

Allen, Grant, 'Falling in Love', *Fortnightly Review* 40 (1886), 452–62.
—— 'The Girl of the Future', *Universal Review* 25 (7 May 1890), 49–64.
—— *The Woman Who Did* (1895) (Oxford: Oxford University Press, 1995). Introduction by Sarah Wintle. Useful literary and historical context to the novel; an astute, balanced reading, with emphasis on the heroine's relationship to the New Woman debates.
—— *A Splendid Sin* (London: F. V. White and Co., 1896).
Brooke, Emma Frances, *A Superfluous Woman* (London: William Heinemann, 1894).
—— *Life the Accuser* (3 vols.) (London: William Heinemann, 1896).
Caffyn, Mannington Katherine ('Iota'), *A Yellow Aster* (London: Hutchinson and Co., 1894).
—— *A Comedy in Spasms* (London: Hutchinson and Co., 1895).
Caird, Mona, 'Marriage', *Westminster Review*, 130:2 (Aug. 1888), 186–201.
—— *The Daughters of Danaus* (1894) ed. Margaret Morganroth Gullette (New York: The Feminist Press at the City University of New York, 1989). Her reappraisal of Caird as a radical feminist rightly brings attention to this important but neglected critic of the era. Provides biographical material, and analysis of Caird's other novels.
—— *The Morality of Marriage and Other Essays on the Status and Destiny of Woman* (London: George Kedway, 1897).
—— 'Does Marriage Hinder a Woman's Development?'(1899), reproduced in *The Daughters of Danaus*, ed. Margaret Morganroth Gullette (New York: The Feminist Press at the City University of New York, 1989).
Cholmondeley, Mary, *Red Pottage* (London: Edward Arnold, 1899).
Chothia, Jean (ed.), *The New Woman and Other Emancipated Woman Plays* (Oxford: Oxford University Press, 1998). Contains Sidney Grundy, *The New Woman* (1894), Arthur Wing Pinero, *The Notorious Mrs*

Ebbsmith (1895), Elizabeth Robins, *Votes for Women!* (1907), and St. John Hankin, *The Last of the De Mullins* (1908). There is a useful introduction by Chothia and explanatory notes.

Corelli, Marie, *The Sorrows of Satan* (1895) (Oxford: Oxford University Press, 1996). With a useful introduction by Peter Keating including discussion of the literary market and a balanced analysis of Corelli's satire of moral and artistic values.

Cross(e), Victoria (Annie Sophie Cory), *The Woman Who Didn't* (London: John Lane, 1895).

—— 'Theodora: A Fragment', *Yellow Book* (1895), reproduced in Elaine Showalter (ed.), *Daughters of Decadence: Women Writers of the Fin de Siècle* (London: Virago, 1993).

—— *Anna Lombard* (1901) (London: John Long, 1902).

—— *Anna Lombard* (1901) (ed.) Gail Cunningham (Birmingham: University of Birmingham Press, 2003).

Darcy, Ella, *Monochromes* (1895) (London: Garland Press, 1977).

Dixon, Ella Hepworth, *The Story of a Modern Woman* (1894) (London: John Lane, 1895).

Dowie, Menie Muriel, *Gallia* (1895) ed. Helen Small (London: Everyman, 1995). This edition has some biographical detail which is brought to bear on the work. An exposition situates Dowie's discussion of emotional psychology and sexual attraction in relation to Havelock Ellis and to Francis Galton, and highlights the wit and authorial irony in the treatment of these subjects.

Egerton, George (Mary Chavelita Dunne), *Keynotes and Discords* (1893) Martha Vicinus (ed.) (London: Virago Press, 1983). Introduction by Vicinus emphasizes the modernity and daring of the stories in the literary culture of the period.

—— 'A Lost Masterpiece', *Yellow Book i* (1894), 189–96.

—— *Symphonies* (London: John Lane, 1897).

—— *Rosa Amorosa: The Love Letters of a Woman* (London: Grant Richards, 1901).

Fitzsimmons, Linda and Viv Gardner (eds.), *New Woman Plays* (London: Methuen, 1991). Contains Florence Bell and Elizabeth Robins, *Alan's Wife*; Cecily Hamilton, *Diana of Dobson's*; Elizabeth Baker, *Chains*; Githa Sowerby, *Rutherford and Son*. There is a useful introduction and a head note to each play.

Gissing, George, *New Grub Street* (1891) (London: Penguin, 1985).

—— *The Odd Women* (London: William Heinemann, 1893).

Grand, Sarah (Frances Elizabeth McFall), *Ideala: A Study from Life* (1888) (London: William Heinemann, 1889).

—— *The Heavenly Twins* (1893) (Ann Arbor: University of Michigan Press, 1992). Introduction by Carol A. Senf which makes links between the life and work with details drawn from Gillian Kersley's autobiography, and with discussion of the contemporary reception of the novel.

—— *The Beth Book* (1897; reprint of 1898 edn.) ed., Sally Mitchell (Bristol: Thoemmes Press, 1994). Mitchell provides a general introduction to New Woman fiction, the woman movement and its relationship to our own times. Her reading highlights Grand's response to the anti-vivisection movement and its relationship to the Contagious Diseases Act, and an analysis of Grand's unusual treatment of girlhood and female adolescent sexuality.

—— 'The Undefinable: A Fantasia' (1908), reproduced in Elaine Showalter (ed.), *Daughters of Decadence: Feminist Fiction at the Fin de Siècle* (London: Virago, 1993), 262–87.

—— *Adnam's Orchard: A Prologue* (London: William Heinemann, 1912).

Heilmann, Ann, *Sex, Social Purity and Sarah Grand*, Volume 3, *Selected Shorter Writings* (London: Routledge , 2000).

—— and Stephanie Forward (eds.), *Sex, Social Purity and Sarah Grand*, Volume 1: *Journalistic Writings and Contemporary Reception* (London: Routledge, 2000).

Lee, Vernon (Violet Paget), *Hauntings: Fantastic Stories* (London: William Heinemann, 1890).

—— *Vanitas: Polite Stories* (London: William Heinemann, 1892).

—— *The Snake Lady and Other Stories* ed., Horace Gregory (New York: Grove Press, 1954).

Nordau, Max, *Degeneration* (1895) (London: University of Nebraska Press, 1993).

Paston, George (Emily Morse Symonds), *A Modern Amazon* (2 vols.) (London: Osgood and McIlvaine, 1894).

—— *A Writer of Books (A Tale)* (1898) (Chicago: Academy Chicago, 1999).

Richardson, Angelique (ed.), *Women Who Did: Stories by Men and Women, 1890–1914* (London: Penguin, 2002). An anthology which includes Caird, Kate Chopin, Grand and Oscar Wilde, with excellent chronology, bibliography and background.

Robins, Elizabeth, *Way Stations* (New York: Dodd and Mead, 1913).

Schreiner, Olive (Ralph Iron, pseud.) *The Story of an African Farm* (1883) (London: Penguin, 1995).

—— *Dreams* (1890) ed., Elisabeth Jay (Birmingham: University of Birmingham, 2003).

—— *Dream Life and Real Life* (reprint of 1909 edition) (Chicago: Academy, 1981).

—— *Woman and Labour* (1911) (London: Virago, 1988).

—— *From Man to Man, Or Perhaps Only . . .* (1926) (London: Virago, 1982).

Scullion, Adrienne (ed.) *Female Playwrights of the Nineteenth Century* (London: Everyman, 1996). Amongst other plays it contains Mrs Henry Wood, *East Lynne* (1874), Florence Bell and Elizabeth Robins, *Alan's Wife* (1893), and a comic play by John Oliver Hobbes (Pearl Craigie), *The Ambassador* (1898).

Showalter, Elaine (ed.), *Daughters of Decadence: Women Writers of the Fin de Siècle* (London: Virago, 1993). Anthology of short stories which includes Olive Schreiner, Vernon Lee, Victoria Cross and Edith Wharton.

Syrett, Netta, *Nobody's Fault* (London: John Lane, 1896).

Webb, Beatrice, *My Apprenticeship* (1926) (Harmondsworth: Penguin, 1971).

—— *The Diaries of Beatrice Webb*, ed. Norman and Jeanne MacKenzie (London: Virago, 2000).

SECONDARY TEXTS

Criticism

Ardis, Ann L., *New Women, New Novels, Feminism and Early Modernism* (London: Rutgers University Press, 1990). This study focuses on the Edwardian period and the relationship of innovative New Woman writing to literary modernism.

Bjørhovde, Gerd, *Rebellious Structures: Women Writers and the Crisis of the Novel 1880–1900* (Oslo: Norwegian University Press, 1987). This insightful study focuses on how women writers transformed the form and narrative structure of the novel.

Burdett, Carolyn, *Olive Schreiner and the Process of Feminism* (Basingstoke: Palgrave, 2000). Comprehensive biographical details and readings of her works embedded in social, political, and scientific contexts.

Burnett, John (ed.), *Useful Toil: Autobiographies of Working People from the 1820s to the 1920s* (London: Allen Lane, 1974).

Cunningham, Gail, *The New Woman and the Victorian Novel* (London: Macmillan, 1978). Early feminist study which considers the New Woman fiction in relation to the novel of her male contemporaries.

Gardner, Viv, 'Women and Writing at the Fin de Siècle' in Marion Shaw (ed.), *An Introduction to Women's Writing from the Middle Ages to the Present Day* (London: Prentice Hall, 1998).

—— and Susan Rutherford (eds.), *The New Woman and her Sisters* (Hemel Hempstead: Harvester Wheatsheaf, 1992).

Heilmann, Ann, *New Woman Fiction: Women Writing First Wave Feminism* (Basingstoke: Macmillan, 2000). Traces the relationship between the fiction and thought of the turn of the century women's movement with that of the later, and second-wave feminist theory. Perceptive analysis of a wide range of texts on diverse themes from cross-dressing to the syphilis plot.

Holbrook Jackson, *The Eighteen Nineties: A Review of Art and Ideas at the Close of the Nineteenth Century* (Brighton: Harvester Press, 1976).

Ingram, Angela and Daphne Patai, *Rediscovering Forgotten Radicals: British Women Writers 1889–1939* (London: University of North Carolina Press, 1993).

Kranidis, Rita S., *Subversive Discourse* (Basingstoke: Macmillan, 1995). Analysis of New Woman fiction in terms of form, aesthetics, and cultural position in the literary market.

Ledger, Sally, *The New Woman Fiction and Feminism at the Fin de Siècle* (Manchester: Manchester University Press, 1997). New Woman lives and fiction are grouped in relation to key cultural contexts including imperialism and socialism. Readings of a wide range of writers including Hume Clapperton, Egerton, Caird and Schreiner.

—— (ed.), *Keynotes and Discords* (1893) (Birmingham: University of Birmingham, 2003). Ledger's excellent introduction provides interesting biographical material. Analysis of motherhood and the aestheticized sexuality in the stories detail Egerton's experimentalism and argue the importance of her status as a modern short-story writer.

McDonagh, Josephine, *Child Murder and British Culture, 1720–1900* (Cambridge: Cambridge University Press, 2003).

Mangum, Teresa, *Married, Middlebrow and Militant: Sarah Grand and the New Woman Novel* (Ann Arbor: Michigan University Press, 1998). Combines extensive biography with criticism. Detailed discussion of works throughout Grand's long career look at her relationship to a number of contemporary movements and ideologies, including eugenics and land reform.

Manos, Nikki Lee and Meri-Jane Rochelson (eds.), *Transforming Genres: New Approaches to British Fiction of the 1890s* (New York: St. Martin's Press, 1994). Includes an essay on Grand's modernist aesthetics.

Marks, Patricia, *Bicycles, Bangs and Bloomers: The New Woman in the Popular Press* (Lexington: University Press of Kentucky, 1990). This study examines the New Woman as consumer, campaigner and comic icon, with illustrations and satirical material from *Punch*.

Miller, Jane Eldridge, *Rebel Women: Feminism, Modernism and the Edwardian Novel* (London: Virago, 1994). This study looks mostly at Edwardian novels and their influence on the Georgians. It discusses how the feminism of the 1890s and beyond made a key contribution to modernist aesthetics.

Nelson, Carolyn Christensen, *British Women Fiction Writers of the 1890's* (New York: Twayne Publishers, 1996). Condensed overview of key New Woman novelists of the period, including Grand and Egerton.

Powell, Kerry, *Women and Victorian Theatre* (Cambridge: Cambridge University Press, 1997).

Pykett, Lyn, *The 'Improper' Feminine: The Women's Sensation Novel and the New Woman Writing* (London: Routledge, 1992). Examines the links between 1860s sensation fiction and the developments of the 1890s. Illuminating account which identifies the formal and stylistic qualities of the New Woman writing as eschewing the old realism for developing proto-modernist tendencies, for example in discussion of Grand's *The Beth Book*.

Randolph, Lyssa, 'The Child and the "Genius": New Science in Sarah Grand's *The Beth Book*', *Victorian Review* 26:1 (2000), 64–81.

Richardson, Angelique, *The Eugenization of Love: Darwin, Galton and Late Nineteenth-Century Fictions of Heredity and Eugenics* (Oxford: Oxford University Press, 2003). Traces the development of the reformation of the domestic romance plot through eugenic aspirations with readings of Hardy, Grand, and Egerton.

—— and Chris Willis (eds.), *The New Woman in Fiction and in Fact: Fin de Siècle Feminisms* (London: Palgrave, 2001). This collection of essays succeeds in situating its figures of the New Woman, real and fictive, in relation to debates from masculinity; Hellenism; theatre; consumerism; eugenics and colonialism, and thus emphasizes her diversity and ideological inconsistency.

Robbins, Ruth and Julian Wolfreys (eds.), *Victorian Gothic: Literary and Cultural Manifestations in the Nineteenth Century* (Basingstoke: Palgrave, 2000), 182–200. Robbins's essay on Vernon Lee discusses her use of androgyny in relation to her aestheticism.

Rover, Constance, *Love, Morals and the Feminists* (London: Routledge & Kegan Paul, 1970).

Schaffer, Talia, *The Forgotten Female Aesthetes: Literary Culture in Late-Victorian England* (London: University Press of Virginia, 2000). Study of 'aesthetic' women writers in various literary and cultural forms, such as Vernon Lee, Alice Meynell and Lucas Malet, and the relationship of their work to their male counterparts. This important analysis allows an instructive comparison with the contrasting aesthetics and polemicism of the New Woman writers.

Showalter, Elaine (ed.), *Speaking of Gender* (London: Routledge, 1989). Includes an essay by Carol Barash, 'Virile Womanhood: Olive Schreiner's Narratives of a Master Race', 269–81.

Tusan, Michelle Elizabeth, 'Inventing the New Woman: Print Culture and Identity Politics During the Fin de Siècle', *Victorian Periodicals Review*, 31:2 (Summer 1998), 169–82.

Biography

Burnham Bloom, Abigail (ed.), *A Bio-Bibliographical Critical Sourcebook* (London: Aldwych Press, 2000). Includes an entry on Mona Caird, 99.

Gunn, Peter, *Vernon Lee: Violet Paget, 1856–1935* (London: Oxford University Press, 1964).

John, Angela V., *Elizabeth Robins: Staging a Life, 1862–1952* (London: Routledge, 1995).

Kersley, Gillian, *Darling Madame: Sarah Grand and Devoted Friend* (London: Virago, 1983). Biographical study incorporating the correspondence between Grand and friend, Gladys Singers Bigger, in the early twentieth century.

Background reading

Bland, Lucy, *Banishing the Beast: English Feminism and Sexual Morality 1885–1914* (London: Penguin, 1995). History of feminist campaigns on sexuality and their relationship to other projects such as the suffrage. Excellent background reading for an understanding of New Woman fiction.

Felski, Rita, *The Gender of Modernity* (London: Harvard University Press, 1995).

Flint, Kate, *The Woman Reader 1837–1914* (Oxford: Clarendon Press, 1993).

Greenslade, William, *Degeneracy, Culture and the Novel, 1880–1940* (Cambridge: Cambridge University Press, 1994).

Heilmann, Ann (ed.), *The Late-Victorian Marriage Question: A Collection of Key New Woman Texts* (5 vols.) (London: Routledge/Thoemmes Press, 1998).

Holmes, Ann Sumner and Claudia Nelson, (eds.), *Maternal Instincts: Visions of Motherhood and Sexuality in Britain 1875–1925* (Basingstoke: Macmillan Press, 1997).

Ledger, Sally and Roger Luckhurst (eds.), *The Fin de Siècle: A Reader in Cultural History c.1880–1900* (Oxford: Oxford University Press, 2000). Wide-ranging selection of extracts reproduced from contemporary reviews and articles on themes of anarchism; degeneration; metropolis; scientific naturalism; spiritualism.

——, —— (eds.) *Cultural Politics at the Fin de Siècle* (Cambridge: Cambridge University Press, 1995). Includes essay by Laura Chrisman, 'Empire, "Race" and Feminism at the Fin de Siècle: The Work of George Egerton and Olive Schreiner', 45–65.

Parsons, Deborah L., *Streetwalking the Metropolis: Women, the City and Modernity* (Oxford: Oxford University Press, 2000). Literary texts that figure are largely post 1900. This study has important theoretical discussion of women writers' relationship to modernism, and in particular the figure of the *flâneur*.

Pykett, Lyn, *Engendering Fictions: The English Novel in the Early Twentieth Century* (London: Edward Arnold, 1995).

—— (ed.), *Reading Fin de Siècle Fictions* (London: Longman, 1996).

Richardson, Angelique, *Love and Eugenics in the Late Nineteenth Century: Rational Reproduction and the New Woman* (Oxford: Oxford University Press, 2003).

Rubinstein, David, *Before the Suffragettes: Women's Emancipation in the 1890s* (Brighton: Harvester, 1986). Background on the period includes information on Grand's relationship with New Woman peers.

Showalter, Elaine, *Sexual Anarchy: Gender and Culture at the Fin de Siècle* (London: Bloomsbury, 1990).

Stokes, John (ed.), *Fin de Siècle / Fin du Globe: Fears and Fantasies of the Late Nineteenth Century* (London: Macmillan, 1992). Rich material on cultural anxieties about degeneration and morbidity and their representation.

Strachey, Ray, *The Cause: A Short History of the Women's Movement* (1936) (London: Virago, 1978). A classic account of the suffrage movement by one who was an active campaigner for women's rights.

Tickner, Lisa, *The Spectacle of Women: Images of the Suffrage Campaign, 1907–1914* (London: Chatto & Windus, 1987).

Vicinus, Martha, *Independent Women: Work and Community for Single Women, 1850–1920* (London: Virago, 1985).

Walkowitz, Judith R., *City of Dreadful Delight: Narratives of Sexual Danger in Late-Victorian London* (London: Virago Press, 1992).

Ware, Vron, *Beyond the Pale: White Women, Racism and History* (London: Verso, 1992). Considers the involvement of women's rights campaigners in imperialism and colonialism.

Index

Note: literary works are indexed under authors' names

Printed and bound by CPI Group (UK) Ltd, Croydon, CR0 4YY

13/04/2025

14656582-0004